DEEP PLAY

PAUL PRITCHARD

DEEP PLAY

Climbing the world's most dangerous routes

FOREWORD BY JOHN MIDDENDORF

VERTEBRATE PUBLISHING

Vertebrate Publishing, Sheffield
www.v-publishing.co.uk

DEEP PLAY
PAUL PRITCHARD

This paperback edition first published in 2012 by Vertebrate Publishing.

VERTEBRATE PUBLISHING
Crescent House, 228 Psalter Lane, Sheffield S11 8UT.
www.v-publishing.co.uk

First published in Britain and America in 1997 by
Bâton Wicks Publications, London and The Mountaineers, Seattle.

This book is a work of non-fiction based on the life, experiences and recollections
of Paul Pritchard. In some limited cases the names of people, places, dates and sequences
or the detail of events have been changed solely to protect the privacy of others.
The author has stated to the publishers that, except in such minor respects not affecting
the substantial accuracy of the work, the contents of the book are true.

A CIP catalogue record for this book is available from the British Library.

ISBN: 978-1-906148-58-4 (Paperback)
ISBN: 978-1-906148-59-1 (Ebook)
10 9 8 7 6 5 4 3 2 1

Every effort has been made to obtain the necessary permissions with reference to copyright material, both illustrative and quoted. We apologise for any omissions in this respect
and will be pleased to make the appropriate acknowledgements in any future edition.

Designed by Nathan Ryder, typeset in Arno Pro by Jane Beagley, Vertebrate Graphics Ltd.
www.v-graphics.co.uk

Printed and bound in the UK by T.J. International Ltd, Padstow, Cornwall.

The purpose of the ladders is to convey the searchers to the niches.
Those whom these entice no longer climb simply to get clear of the ground.

— Samuel Beckett

CONTENTS

ACKNOWLEDGEMENTS

Firstly I would like to thank Maggie Body, my editor, for doing such a fine job with the text. I am also indebted to John Middendorf for honouring me with his Foreword and to Andy Parkin for his wonderfully enigmatic drawings which embellish the text. Then I must thank Harold Wooley for teaching me how to climb and ruining my academic career. I am deeply indebted to Gill Kent for having so much faith in my writing for so long. Thanks too to Gwion Hughes, George Smith, Noel Craine, Jim Perrin and all my other mates for their reading and criticism and Greg Rimmer for his work with my manuscript. The photographic spreads have been strengthened by the contributions of Tony Kay, Bill Hatcher, Iwan Jones, Simon Yates, Ben Wintringham, Ken Wilson, Sean Smith and Alun Hughes, to whom I owe thanks. My earnest thanks must go to Marko Prezelj for his work on the cover photo too which was lost a long time since.

A thank you also to: the MEF and the BMC without whose financial help some of our trips might not have happened; Ben Lyon for his continued support for my pie in the sky schemes; Glenn Robbins for saving my life and Olly Saunders for finding us; Nick Kekus for saving it again and Robert Hester and Nick Burring for coping so well on that awful day; Lochaber and Valley Rescue Teams and the Holyhead lifeboat crew for doing their jobs so faultlessly; all my friends I have lived and climbed with and who have given me the raw material to write about in this book. I would also like to show my gratitude to my parents for letting me be what I wanted to be. Finally, thank you Celia Bull for the love, the laughs, the tears, the support – for sharing the adventure. Cheers Ed, Philip and Teo. My book is dedicated to those times.

This new edition is also dedicated to my father for teaching me the meaning of freedom.

FOREWORD

by JOHN MIDDENDORF

Shortly after Paul Pritchard extended the honour to me of writing the foreword for his book, I had the opportunity to catch up with him for a climb of The Old Man of Hoy, a five-hundred foot sandstone stack on the sea cliffs of the Orkney Islands, a climb which for me has been a lifelong ambition. In fine Scottish weather, a drenching rain and fierce wind, we crouched on tiny stances far off the deck and chatted about the state of affairs. "Bit of a job lately," he told me of his most recent employment. "Been rappelling down a nuclear processing plant, sweeping out the dust in dark, deep chambers. Haven't felt well since the work ended." Paul is a natural story teller and always has an interesting tale, generally told in understated terms. We discussed different climbs around the world that we've mutually appreciated, and watched the sea waves pound on the rocky pedestal below us. It was good fun on the Old Man with Paul, terrified as I was after months at a desk, climbing the exposed, wet, and overhanging 5.8 and 5.10 crack pitches. We reached the summit toward dusk and shared the airy perch with dozens of calm puffins, who showed us their dance on the rims of the stack with magnificent hummingbird-like flight in the stiff ocean winds. I reflected on Paul's book and on the emotive side of climbing, and how an essay of such moments is a treat for the times when we are bound to the reality of terra firma, towards which we soon began to descend.

Although I had never before climbed with him, I was nevertheless not surprised when I noticed Paul's calm nerve on the stone. He belongs to an imaginative and talented group of individuals who I have had the pleasure to meet all over the world; people who share little in terms of cultural backgrounds, yet who have a common bond in their eclectic pursuit of a particular aspect of climbing. It is a group of folks who have honed a bold climbing style and who share an interest in the same thin strips of rock rearing up the most magnificent and giant rock walls on our planet. It is people who, in Paul's own words, share the experience of "the wind and the waiting" in the mountains. It is interesting how climbers with diverse languages, meeting perhaps in the Mountain Room Bar in Yosemite or maybe in a remote campsite on a tributary of the Baltoro Glacier, will discuss in detail each feature of a particular unclimbed line on a mountain which is thousands of miles away. The discussions share a common thread: a desire to find a wild place where climbing is the most intense and pure.

Paul's own realisations of such desire are on some of the world's biggest rock faces: Meru, the Central Tower of Paine, El Capitan, Mt Asgard. He captures the common essence of these climbs in stories of his adventures of bold climbs, long climbs, cold climbs, and insane climbs. In fine British tradition of pushing the limits of human endeavour on difficult rock routes in the mountains, Paul's climbs add to a rich history of British climbing which includes the original ascent of Trango Tower in 1976 by Martin Boysen, Mo Anthoine, Joe Brown and Malcolm Howells, the alpine-style push up the Golden Pillar of Spantik in 1987 by Mick Fowler and Victor Saunders, and the bold foray on Cave Man on the Cuerno de Paine by Twid Turner and Louise Thomas in 1993. Many of these climbers cut their teeth on the cliffs of North Wales and wild sea cliffs of Gogarth on routes of unmatched on-sight first ascent standards, and later took their bold techniques into the mountains.

The routes at Gogarth have always fascinated me – many times in my twenty-five years of climbing, I have seen the fear in climbers' eyes while talking about their hands-on experience with Gogarth routes. Preserved from the modern trend of grid-bolting due to the general rejection of bolts on the sea cliffs (an attitude enhanced possibly from the fact that any bolts would corrode instantly in the saline sea air) and safe from the current view that regards difficulty solely by its number, Gogarth has been the arena of several generations of the world's boldest routes. Paul's route Super Calabrese on the Red Wall, which he climbed in 1986, represents the extreme of ground-up climbing. The Gogarth guide says of the Red Wall, "This superb orange wall gives open climbing of a serious and often precarious nature. None of the routes should be treated without respect, the situation contributing its fair share of intimidation." In the story Lost in the Broccoli Garden, Paul reflects after a Gogarth pitch, "I wasn't experiencing the anti-cipated satisfaction of completing such a frightening pitch. It was numbness." The guidebook lists the route with the notation, "a contender for the poorest belay on Gogarth". He explains the delicate experience of finding oneself in a crazy location, dependent only on one's mettle and driven by adrenaline, and finding the body and mind take over for the climb.

Paul Pritchard's tales are not only of the extreme intensity of bold routes, but also of the essential nature of the lifestyle. The book begins with "Fire Starter" a background of his childhood and the political and social atmo-sphere in which he grew up. The stories give insight to the motives of climbing extraordinary climbs, and tell of Paul and his mates as youths getting into the vertical in a world without limits, rife with lawlessness and little regard for personal safety, and with an immutable code of retaining the purest climbing style. He tells of a life of irreverence and a tad of decadence, that seeks the experience of utter dependence on craftiness and motivation. These stories link the common theme of the spirit's search for a purity of desire.

Deep Play is a collection of reflections on people and places, and of stories of deaths of close friends, and the experience of a brush with mortality. The author's sensitivity in seeing the true nature of his friends is captured spot-on with tales of other climbers: José Pepe Chaverri, Silvo Karo, Philip Lloyd, Teo Plaza, and others. The book is an analysis of a climber's mind, with the full realm of emotion. It's about sharing with new friends, and climbing new things and being in new places, on adventures where climbing the mountain is only half of the experience.

It is a rare and inspiring thing that such tales of intensity, joy and suffering have been put onto paper, rather than the usual event of the magic being lost via a rough translation from mind to paper, or mere lack of documentation before the essence leaves the consciousness. Thank you, Paul, for reminding us about that magic, and congratulations for your finest timeless testpiece yet.

JOHN MIDDENDORF
San Francisco, 1997

Dossing in The Land of the Midnight Sun, I didn't give a stuff about how much climbing rocks could teach me. I couldn't care less that this uncomplicated life would instil in me an unshakeable knowledge that I had my own place and voice in the world. That it would prepare me for the pain to come was but a lagniappe, which would equip me with the presence and will to heal. At that time I felt there were only two things in my life: me and the rock.

However, pertaining to *Deep Play*, this dedicated existence furnished me with the follow through to realise my dreams. And one such dream was this book. It is only now, from a twenty-first century perspective. that I understand just how important a record of a great era – perhaps the last great era – of British climbing *Deep Play* is.

The eighties was a unique decade in British climbing: a time of flux. It was a time of economic depression and special was the fact that it was the first depression truly buoyed up by a welfare system. For climbing culture the eighties didn't just mean shit jumpers, bad barnets and god-awful tights. It was an age floating between more prosperous times. The seventies was notable as a climbing superstar culture with big names such as Doug Scott, Dougal Haston, Alex MacIntyre and Chris Bonington, who undertook major sponsored expeditions, the likes of which had not been seen since the first ascent of Everest – Barclays Bank put up one hundred thousand pounds for the Everest South West Face Expedition in 1975. The nineties saw the rise of the sharp-cut professional: Houlding, MacLeod, Cool and Emmett, an era which has continued to this day.

In a sense, climbing, at least for the adventure, lost its way in the nineties. However, the on-sight bold ascent has returned in the last few years with climbers on-sighting the 'headpoints' of the 1980s and making audacious first ascents on rock and in the Mountains. Dave MacLeod's *Echo Wall* and many of Leo Houlding's ascents on rock and in the mountains are examples of this. However, it is American Dean Potter's B.A.S.E. solo of *Deep Blue Sea* on the North Face of the Eiger that really does show the future of climbing.

In *Deep Play* I mention the economic hardship, the huge rates of unemployment and the vast well of creativity that came with it. I also mention the distaste: some people simply felt that we should get jobs. With hindsight it is interesting to note that lots of artists made good in that time. Indeed, celebrated author Hanif Kureshi, who garnered a CBE in 2008, began his artistic career on the dole in the 1980s. One thing is clear: all the UK climbers of the eighties have one person to thank for giving them this golden opportunity: Margaret Thatcher.

As for my book: there are moments of naive pomposity within its pages. Yet far from being embarrassed about this, I believe these moments reveal an honesty that I would have trouble finding in my writing nowadays.

I opened the book with, "I am definitely a climber who writes." The judges at the Boardman Tasker Prize thought I was being swell headed; in fact, I remember John Porter translating my statement to, "I was born to write about climbing." I simply and innocently assumed too much from my readers whom I thought would have read their Drummond and their Child, who it is said of both that; it is not clear whether they are writers who climb or climbers who write. So the statement was my way of supplicating myself to these great writers.

Finally, I stand by the name of the book even though it could be seen to be self-indulgent. Eighteenth Century philosopher Jeremy Bentham, who coined the term *Deep Play*, describes it as a game with stakes so high that no rational person would engage in it. Yet most climbers would describe themselves as rational. Wouldn't you? It is precisely because your life matters to you, not the contrary, that you take risks. When you go out to climb a new route and publicly reveal such stakes there is an awful lot to lose. You risk your status, your pride, your dignity, your masculinity (I can only speak for males on this motivation) ... but most of all your life.

PAUL PRITCHARD
Tasmania
September 2012

PLAYING THE SYSTEM

I am definitely a climber who writes. I've always written about what I've done and how I felt about myself and those I went with. I have come home from trips with battered books full of scribblings, half of it illegible, self-indulgent babble. At home I have mulled things over, added reflection to the gut reaction of my diaries, and somehow ended up with finished pieces. But the rock has always come first.

Illness on return from trips has allowed me the time to create and smashed bones have also been kind to me, holding me back from my normal unquestioning frenzy of activity and forcing me to sit and think. Indeed I would not have found the time to put these writings together had I not suffered a broken back in Scotland. I used to be so single-minded. Girlfriends and great things I could have done were left behind as I kept searching for the perfect climb. Then, after I fell at Gogarth and momentarily died, I had so many questions to ask the night. I couldn't make any sense of it all and I began writing as an exorcism. At first I thought that moment of drowning felt too good and this terrified me but, as I wrote, I began to make some twisted sense of it all.

Most importantly, the trauma of the events which are documented in this book have helped me to grow and have taught me valuable, very personal lessons. Falling at Gogarth revealed to me my position within humankind; as unimportant as anyone else. That insight allows me to treat all others as equal to myself more readily. There I also learned that death can be painless, yes, but more than that, utterly sublime. This simple knowledge has helped me reconcile the sad thoughts of friends who have died in pain – Ed and Philip and Teo – though it also revealed to me that death really was the end and that there is no time to waste in this short term that we have.

Joe Tasker and Menlove Edwards are two people who have inspired me to put pen to paper, Tasker for his honesty and Edwards for his sensitivity. I will never forget being shocked, as I first read *Savage Arena*, at the vivid description of the arguments which Tasker and Boardman had on their ascents, arguments which many climbers would try to hide for fear of causing offence and embarrassment. And the admission of the fact that their motivations often came from the less admirable corners of their psyche. What can I say about Edwards? Only that, for me, he transforms his insight into nature and the society around him onto paper better than any climber I know of. Nothing or no one seemed able to disguise anything from him. I admit to wanting to emulate their traits but, I hope, I keep my own style.

This is not a simple autobiography. I have tried to give a whole image of the existence and psyche of a climber from my generation, for I do not see myself as so unique within it, though of course A Game One Climber Played and other moments in the book are very personal to me. This is why some of the chapters appear altered from what has been published in magazines. A magazine that readers dip into, not knowing what kind of excitement they are looking for, and so only happening across a piece of your life, is not the place for such intimate subjects. In a book, on the other hand, readers must go out and find, already knowing that they want to learn about you or read what you have to say.

The rock climber who learns his craft and then makes the transition to the mountains is less common now than in previous eras and so my stories of trips aren't perhaps so typical of my genre. But there are a number of us who, even though we might not have experienced it first hand, have roots in the past, have a great respect for the old pioneers and the evolution of our climbing lives would seem to mirror theirs to some extent.

My generation of climbers, the ones who began making their impact in the eighties, had their own peculiarities that set them apart from other generations. These differences were a result of social circumstances in the UK at the time. We had time on our hands and an opportunity to forfeit the worker's life and just go climbing. Some called us selfish. It was a world which produced a crop of British climbers in the early to mid-eighties who showed the world how it was done. I wouldn't be so bold as to rank myself alongside eighties sport climbers – Myles, Moon, or others who were of that new 'leisure class' – but in my own way I feel I've given something to climbing in Britain. I have threaded lines up mountains and sea cliffs and shown others where to go. It wasn't all selfish on my part; I have created steep, mind-testing challenges for climbers to stretch themselves out on. Asgard's velvet smooth wall, Paine's mile-long knife-blade crack, Meru's Shark Fin I needed to try. They were only imaginable for me after a decade of living for the rock every day, blowing off everything else. My need to get stronger, to use all my time struggling towards my dreams, even though I had no private wealth, is what some found disagreeable.

There was a letter sent in to an American climbing magazine once deriding me for "lacking in character" because I indulged my passion "at the expense of the British tax-payer by claiming the munificent British Dole". There are many of this opinion when it comes to judging the out of work. I would like a little room to explain the system I grew up in. I would like to give those people a portrait of the Lancashire of my youth.

In '79, after Callaghan lost, it could be said that the blanket attitude of the young began to change. By '83 there were 4,000,000 men and women unemployed, workers' morale was sinking. Companies won contracts by paying their workers less money for longer hours. The dismantling of the heavy industries and the move toward communications and finance sucked the life out of the industrial areas. This led to a widespread loss of respect for the Conservatives in my home, a northern mill town, which still endures today. To the north of Manchester the miners' strike brought communities to tears, as the collieries of Brackley, Ashtons Field and Hulton stood silent. But, for us youngsters, this was now the land of opportunity, the government told us anything could be ours. We were free to gamble, but if we failed, we would be at the bottom of the heap. When it came time to leave school most of my friends either signed on as unemployed or went on government job creation schemes. The ones that signed on had free time to develop sometimes obscure skills that seemed at first to have no use to the community. Later this would be seen not to be the case as, throughout the country, champion runners and cyclists and famous painters and writers emerged.

At Hulton some of our neighbours went through the picket lines to work because their families needed food. They compromised principles, though they agreed with the strikers' cause. Moral decay had been forced. Nationally this went even further as armaments became one of the biggest industries of the UK, our most marketable product, and who the buyer was didn't matter. How do climbers fit into this you may wonder? Out of the ashes of this social, economic and moral turmoil the full time climber rose like some scruffy, bedraggled phoenix to push the boundaries of what was possible on our crags, quarries and sea cliffs.

There had already been full-timers for a while then. Bancroft, a gritstone cult hero, was probably the original dole climber back in '77, followed by such masters as Allen and Fawcett who gave so much to us younger climbers. When I stood at the bottom of Beau Geste or Master's Edge I could see them moving just as I wanted to move. I wondered if I could ever be like them. Many then could still use university as an excuse to climb. Grants were good and it gave lots of free time, and a chance for MacIntyre and Rouse to become such great mountaineers. Later, as grants decreased, students even had to work their summer holidays (as they still do) and the university life became less appealing to the dedicated climber.

As the young athletes strove to ascend wilder and wilder rock climbs the endeavour became more time-consuming. They had to train long and hard to develop the power needed to create these masterpieces. These climbers paid little thought to the politicans in Westminster, who were inadvertently creating an environment most suitable for the serious climber – with so many unemployed it was easy to sign on. How could they prove you weren't actively seeking work if there wasn't any work to be found? And it became easy to justify too; you could go out to the sea cliffs self-righteous in the knowledge that another was working and feeding his family as a result of your sacrifice! We did look for work, me and my friends, but we were not going to go into a factory after the freedom we had tasted. That no jobs were ever offered to us by the job centre, as was the system, only reflected the economic circumstances of the country, especially in the rural areas of Wales. So why should I not use my time to go climbing? It now seems ironic that my passion contributed to the transformation of the gigantic Dinorwig slate quarries, the scar left after the community was near fatally wounded by its closure. Together we unemployed bums created, from what was once a thriving place of work, and then a vast, silent ugly space, a place of leisure for the weekend climber. And it was hard, dangerous graft, let me tell you, the clearing of loose rock and the drilling, just like the quarrymen had once done. Harder than any desk job I used to think.

But the dole handout or the government climbing grant, as we called it, paid very little. For my first two years as a full-timer, living in the Stoney Middleton wood shed or in caves around the Peak, I received eighteen pounds a week. I had to buy and sell, borrow and steal to get a rack and feed myself. We lived in the dust on a diet of cold beans and white bread.

They banned us from the pub because we didn't spend enough and they thought we would give the other customers our flu. It was a gamble climbing on the dole, to deprive yourself of all those potential luxuries for the sake of pushing up the grades. Most of my old school mates had cars and girlfriends by then. And what if you didn't make it? What would you do in ten years time if you got injured and you had no education or trade to fall back on? I still wonder. But I don't regret forfeiting the career and the consumer durables.

Some of the route names of those days celebrated the unprecedented situation in which climbing found itself, which couldn't have come about in a more healthy economic state. Doleman, Dole Technician, Dolite, Long Live Rock and Dole. One of the ardent Stoney dossers, Dirty Derek, said he'd vote Tory again to ensure he'd get another four years of Giros! But the dossers have gone now. Their generation only really lasted a decade. A climber on the dole is scum in the eyes of many now. New rules have made it tough to stay signed on for any length of time and to be a traveller, like many US climbers, is not an accepted way to live. They put barriers up in Britain and signs, NO OVERNIGHT PARKING. Now many climbers aspire to wealth and sponsorship and a sporty car as an escape from the trap of conformism. They want to attain what their heros have attained. But neither type, not the doley nor the new professional, ever escapes. They both play the system.

It is acceptable to be a student, to study philosophy or art, and you can receive a meagre grant, but to filter out a little money to create great lines up cliffs is, in the eyes of some, morally wrong. It doesn't quite adhere to the system which we manufactured. What does appear ironic now is that those unemployed, who appeared of no use to the community, having perfected their craft, were seen on the pages of magazines and in advertisements. They were transformed into heroes who helped to sell the equipment the manufacturers were producing and so, inadvertently, became an indispensable part of the system they thought they had dropped out of.

To live the life we chose we rode on the wealth of others, just like the explorers of old and these, surely, must command all our respect. Shipton, Tilman, even Darwin made their journeys of discovery using the riches of the empire – from exploitation of conquered lands. They were of the original leisure class which will always be with us. They have been around for ever, almost. The working-class climbers slowly came on the scene from the thirties to the fifties. They were hard men who gained fame on the outcrops near their city homes. After the war there were enough jobs for everyone and their ascents could be made in a day or two at the weekend.

As the boom babies grew up job opportunities diminished and the seventies brought the new leisure class, rebels with a rock hard cause. And now, are we heading back to the beginning? You can climb Everest if you have enough cash. Or perhaps you would prefer Antarctica or Irian Jaya? It was said in the eighties that at either end of the economic spectrum there was a leisure class. Through unemployment the poor had the time to have their adventures, albeit on a smaller scale, on the rock outcrops close to their homes. Now, in the nineties, this may still be true but the opportunities open to the lower leisure class would seem to be restricted somewhat when compared to how it was a decade ago.

As the economy of our island grows again and more restrictions are put on our welfare state the unemployed climber is becoming a thing of the past. Now you'll see less and less of our type. I knew some real characters dossing on that Peak District garage forecourt we called The Land of the Midnight Sun. They lived for the rock and material gain never really entered their heads. I think when we opened the door for the new professionals some of those characters slipped out the back.

CRACK

CHAPTER ONE

FIRE-STARTER

I was born on top of the quarry. It was the best place to mess about a kid could ever want. I never had to go to my mates' houses to play, 'cos they would always come here if I said let's go in the quarry. It was a glowing green hole in the moors. It was my Grand Canyon, my Amazon, my centre of the earth and my one million years BC. I had seen Tyranno-saurus fighting with Stegosaurus, flying saucers with deathrays, and even a ghost – a yellow custardy thing. That ghost gave me such bad dreams that I shat in my bed when it drifted across our best room towards me.

If you leaned out of our bathroom window, the cliff went sheer down to the scrappers' yard and me and my mates used to push bits of our garden wall over the edge so the rocks would land and crash on the pile of dead cars and corrugated tin below. We'd count one ... two ... three ... f ... always a little too fast. But then the scrapper would come up and him and my old man would shout at each other. Another good one was to stand and pee over the edge and see if you could see it reach the bottom by leaning out more and more, but you had to have good balance for that. There was one tree that tilted out right over the drop and we would climb it, up into the thin top branches and look straight down a hundred feet.

We could get the whole tree moving like mad if a few of us started swaying. We even made a death swing out over the cliff, but that disappeared one day.

In the dry summer I sometimes nicked a box of Swan Vestas, we always had matches on us, and we would set the grass on fire on top of the cliff. It always got out of control really fast. We tried to put them out, the fires, but we all secretly wanted the whole moor to burn 'cos when it got too big we'd all laugh and betcha whether the fire engines would come or not. When we heard the sirens we'd all get dead excited and run off, but not too far, so we could hide behind a wall and see the fire brigade beating at the grass. But once we got caught after we'd burnt a derelict hospital down and the pig said the arsonist always returns to the scene of the crime. Me, Lloydy and Cooksy were bricking it but they couldn't prove anything. It's just it was the same ones who caught us after we'd tied the elastic across the road and it had twanged their aerial, so they were suspicious.

But down inside the quarry it was all shady and cool and we would get goose bumps as we sat and chewed the white roots of the couch grass which tasted of summer. Heather tickled the backs of our grass-stained legs and we sprinted off, with our hands and feet, up ledgy rocks. To the top of Cleveland's Edge we would go, a thin finger of rock miles high sticking out into the quarry, only three feet wide at the end. We would play tig on it, and if you didn't stand right on the end you were a big girl's blouse. But the ramp up the front was the best dare. We knew a kid had fallen off the top and died but that didn't stop us. The whole gang of us would swarm up, sometimes standing on each other's shoulders to reach the next shelf. In summer the rocks were dusty, but in winter they were green and slippy – and you'd always have soaked keks before you got to the bottom, from the long grass and heather. Once, trying to get onto a ledge that all the others were on, with the rocks all sloping the wrong way, they started lobbing matches at me. I shouted, "Quit it. Quit it!" and after we got on top I hated them. I got my own back another day though, when I set a plastic bag on fire and dropped zippers, that's what we called the dripping plastic, on Sucks' kid brother while he was stuck on a ledge. He hadn't done anything to me but he was the easiest to pick on – even Sucks kicked him in all the time.

My dad used to tell me stories of when he was in the army. Of Egypt, the Pyramids and Petra. Down in the quarry the towers of rock became great sitting Ramases and Sphinx, the mill-wheels spare parts for Egyptian chariots. The slag heaps became burial mounds which I excavated in search of treasure and mummified bodies. I had my tool kit in a canvas satchel, with trowels and brushes for clearing the dirt off potential precious objects, and a ball of string. During one excavation, at the entrance of a definite burial chamber, we found a stack of nude books which we all gathered round, pointing at the pictures and giggling confusedly. We hid them and came back most evenings for kind of club meetings, but when we came back one day someone had nicked them.

My old man didn't like me going to school. He said I would learn more walking on the moors with him. He never really went to school when he was a kid and he said he was better for it. So we'd go off in the early morning with the shotguns along the edge of the hole, shooting at whatever we saw. Besides rabbits, hares and pigeons, we shot blackbirds, peewits, geese and even, once, a fox. We ate everything but the fox tasted horrible. The worst time was when he went mad at me 'cos I looked inside the barrel of the shotgun when it was loaded. "What the bloodyellfire," he shouted, pulling the 12-bore out of my hands. Once, on top of Cleveland's Edge we saw a family of owls, a mother and three babies. We just sat and watched them. We didn't want to shoot them. They were the best things I'd ever seen. After that I got really into watching the birds and didn't want to shoot them any more. A bit later I remember crying when he shot a kestrel. I held it in my hand and it was so soft and still warm. Its blood trickled down my hand.

It was the same kestrel whose eggs I once nicked when me and my brother still had our big collection. It took us ages to work out how to get to the nest. We'd known where it was for ages, miles up the cliff, but only a stupid get would climb down there. But then we nicked some bailing twine from Locker's barn and I was lowered over the edge. It was all grass and loose rocks and the twine dug into my kidneys. At the nest I was mesmerised, the eggs were so perfect. I put them both in separate pockets and scrambled back up with the gang pulling from above. Later we made pinprick holes in each end of the eggs and blew them into a saucer. Then we proudly set them in their right place in the collection, in their bed of sawdust between the thrush egg and the crow's egg.

In the winter-time we lived in Spain. It was great 'cos it meant that I didn't have to go to school. I laughed about all the others back at home in school and here was our Dave and Trace and me doing what we wanted every day, playing on the beach or fishing or adventuring. We lived eleven storeys up in some apartments, right above the cemetery. Sometimes we'd be having our dinner and there'd be a funeral going on down below. Once me and our Dave went exploring in there and saw these dirty hunchbacked men digging up all the graves. There were coffins and piles of bones everywhere. We started to go nearer for a closer look but this grave-digger saw us and picked up a skull and ran at us with it. We started legging it and my heart was beating dead fast and then this skull came bouncing past me. We told our mum and she told us not to go in there again.

Me and our Dave used to fight a lot but he was six years older than me so I always got paggered. But he tormented me so much that I'd get my own back on him by stealing his spends. He got really angry with me once 'cos I had told on him for drawing pictures of people with no clothes on and when mum and dad went out he picked me up and dangled me by the ankles over the balcony. I stopped shouting and wriggling and just went quiet as I stared down for hundreds of feet. He dragged me back over but I didn't cry, I just looked at him, and he said that if I told I would get it.

Back home we had pigs and hens and rabbits, too, and my dad showed us how to slaughter them. My sister wouldn't get involved, but me and our Dave loved it. We killed the rabbits by chopping them on the back of the neck but they didn't always die straight away. The hens were easier, you just twisted their necks and sometimes they would run around with their heads flopping around. Once a year we had to kill our pigs and to save money my dad didn't take them to the slaughter-house. One Sunday morning, dead early, we went up to the pen. The farmer had told dad that if you draw a line with a magic marker between the pig's ears and eyes and hit it spot on with a pick-axe, the thing will die in a second. So my dad crept up to it and whacked the pick into its head, but it went mad and started screaming. It tore the axe out of his hand and ran about the pen. Its howling was like a baby. It was horrible. My dad picked me up and ran out of the pen with me and told me to get the gun. He was worried 'cos he said the bloody neighbours might call the bloody police. I ran like mad back up the steps with the 12-bore and the cartridges. Pinky, that's the name our Trace gave the pig, was still screeching and the axe handle was waving around in the air. My dad loaded the gun, aimed it and fired. He's a good shot, my dad. Pinky shut up straight away and fell on its face and my dad was pleased 'cos he'd shot it right in the heart. We tied a rope around its head and lifted it into a bath for cutting up. As me and our Dave pulled on the rope, dad chopped at Pinky's neck with his Bowie knife and we went flying backwards as its head came off. Our Trace didn't like eating bacon for breakfast after that.

Most of Bolton's joyriders dumped their night's fun in the quarry, too, and we would always be first there to strip off all the useful scrap. Even the windscreens and seats we got for our dens, but we never found a suitcase of dosh in the boot. If they hadn't already been burnt we would set them on fire and run off to hide nearby and watch the black smoke rising. Running through the quarry I cut my knee open on glass. It didn't hurt, but I still cried. The blood tasted of metal. Suddenly I hated the quarry and wanted my mum to wash the cut. Back home in the cool cave of our dining room it took a while for my eyes to get used to the darkness. She put a sticking plaster on my cleaned up knee, ruffled my hair, and got back to top and tailing gooseberries. I limped back out into the heat, proud of my wound, to eat slugs and horse muck for 10p dares off my mates.

We found a brand new shiny rope on the floor behind Cleveland's, and some other stuff, but we just took the rope and sneaked off up our secret path. We made a massive death slide in Bluebell forest which should have been ace but the stupid rope stretched and you hit the ground.

I always saw climbers on the walls. They were just part of the quarry, up there for ages, not moving and shouting signals to each other. It was then that I found out how to make petrol bombs and I loved throwing them off the top of the cliff. There was one time I did something really daft and threw one down at a bunch of climbers. The milk bottle smashed on the cliff face and fire showered down on them. They started pointing and shouting and I ran for it with my heart beating dead fast.

We went back with the stretchy rope and tied it to the top of the cliff face. Then we threw the rest off and went round to the bottom. We swarmed up the rope one at a time, trying to be like the climbers, but it cut into our hands. Then one of the climbers came over with a proper helmet on and everything and said he'd take us up a route. We weren't sure what a route was but he tied the rope around our waists with a proper climber's knot and showed us how to use the cracks and that with our hands and feet. It was loads easier than trying to grab the rope.

We had to leave the big old house when mum and dad split up and go into a flat on the main road in town, above a hairdressers. But I still wagged off school and went up over the moors to the quarry. I took new mates with me though. I'd lost touch with my old ones. Cooksy had moved to another town and Lloydy had killed himself joyriding. He got drunk on cider and nicked a car and when the pigs came after him he hit a tree going dead fast. I can't drive. We'd take cider and drink it as fast as we could and lie in the warm heather 'till late, our mothers wondering where we were. Three days a week the gun club would come to the quarry. Grown Lancashire men dressed as American cops, shades and bomber jackets. They'd chew gum and shoot automatic pistols at cardboard cut-outs of people. When they stopped to change cartridges we'd shout "Waaaaankeeeeers" … and leg it.

We saw a man chasing a woman around the slag heaps and we crawled over to the edge. They lay down behind Cleveland's Edge, amidst the tin cans and whirlpools of crisp packets, and she pulled up her skirt. We watched them doing it for a while, biting our collars to stop the giggles, but shy too, in front of each other, with longing. Then Judd shouted something and we rolled on our backs laughing so much that we couldn't breathe. I saw our house at the end of the quarry with strangers in the garden, and stopped smiling. We walked back along Scout Road, the lovers' lane from where you can see the whole of Manchester, Jodrell Bank space telescope and right across to the Snowdon mountains, where we played spot the used johnny, and where we once saw a car rocking to and fro with a pair of bare feet at the window. I didn't want to go back there. I went to town instead 'cos that's where my new mates hung out. We did loads of shoplifting. We'd nick anything for a laugh and sometimes have to run out of Woolys or somewhere being chased by security, and we'd turn our jackets inside out and our hats around as a disguise. We moved on to half bottles of Bells and hung around the town centre, drunk. We acted like stupid buggers when we were drunk. "When all the lights are flashin' we're goin' Paki bashin'" a bunch of skins were singing. They were old lads, maybe eighteen. I shouted something to them, I don't remember what, and they ran over and swiped me round the head with a bike chain. When I went down they all put the boot in and I woke up in some woods, bruised and all covered in dry blood. I told my mum I'd fallen out of a tree. She always pretended to believe me.

I didn't like the secondary school. I'd never really been to school that much before 'cos we always lived in Spain in the winter and my mum would teach me the stuff I needed to know. The white kids called me Paki because of my tanned skin. They were just jealous. But I did have my mates and we'd wag off together and go and play space invaders or go robbing. So I don't know why I jumped down the stairs. I just looked down the well, four storeys from Mr Wooley's Physics lab, like a spiral tunnel, and slid over. I didn't want to kill myself – more like I did it to live, to prove I could do it. I knew I could do anything and I'd jumped off loads of things for dares. But that wasn't for a dare. Something gripped me as I stared over the edge. Something drew me over and I knew I wouldn't hurt myself. A teacher saw me as I was clambering over the rail and moved to stop me, so I just let go and dropped. I saw his face recede into the distance. The banisters echoed as I bounced between them and my hands ripped as I clutched at them. I remember seeing Wingnut on my way past and trying to shout to him, but my breath was taken. I remember hitting a big grey radiator down in the pool changing area and seeing the red floor tiles for a second, but nothing else. I woke up in hospital. At first I couldn't move. My body was rigid and aching. I trembled. My hands were all torn and bandaged, like after I'd jumped I'd regretted it and was trying to stop myself. I think I do that a lot, throw myself into things and then wish I hadn't. It's hard to believe I didn't break anything and I was back at the school in a few days, but I kept having these breakdowns where I'd start crying and shaking. But everyone wanted to be my mate then and they even put metal studs on all the banisters in the school, like a special memorial to me.

I wasn't good at games and when we had to go on cross-country I'd always throw up, or we'd sneak off to Judd's house, which was on the circuit, and smoke a fag. We got caned for that when they caught us. But then they had this new scheme where we could go rock climbing with Mr Wooley instead of getting killed trying to play rugby. I thought it was great. I hadn't been up to the quarry for ages and every week we did a different climb from the guidebook. I wanted to do every climb in that book, each with its own name and grade, either jamming or chimneying or laybacking. Some of the lads hated it, getting scared and dirty and the midges and everything, but I wanted it to go on loads longer. I loved the taste of that dust from the rock, just like when I was a kid, and I knew these holes like the back of my hand. Now I was sitting on ledges that I could never get to before.

I went and bought a pair of proper rock boots and started traversing around the walls after school. Sometimes I met climbers who would take me up a route on Cleveland's Edge, the climbers called it The Prow, and sometimes I brought my sleeping bag and kipped on top of the crag. I went and looked over the garden wall of our old house, I had to, and they had pulled up the fruit bushes and chopped down the orchard to make a lawn. The giant oak I swung in with my farm mates had been chopped down, and one of those new estates had been built. It made me feel hollow inside, but it was easier to let go of now that they had made it ugly and all the nooks and crannies of adventure had been demolished.

On a summer's day, just before they sent me on the Youth Training Scheme, I was sat in the familiar heather, picking hardened chalk from behind my fingernails with a piece of grass, when I noticed a thin man bobbing along the top of the crag with a sack on his back. He stopped, peered over the edge and then climbed down a smooth overhanging face. I flicked through the guidebook and stopped at the right page: The Grader, E3! I didn't know this sort of climber existed. I saw him another time, with some friends, climbing up and down a leaning wall again and again, with the sack on like last time. I kept my distance, like I was scared of these superclimbers, but they called me over and explained to me that they were training and the bag was full of rocks. John, Tony and Monksy said if I did the same I'd get better, too. That was it. I quit the scheme after fighting with the caretaker of the technical college I was at. He broke my nose with his broom handle. I spent all my time in the quarry, traversing there and back and trying all the problems the superclimbers had shown me. Before long I was going up and down The Grader, too, with my other dole mate, Phil, and a bag of rocks.

At sixteen I was in the Black Dog with the hard guys, nursing tired, bloody hands and supping bitter. Monksy was telling a story of when they were all bouldering, years ago mind, and some kid lobbed a petrol bomb over the crag, right at them. They didn't find him but if they had, they would have given him a right good hiding.

CHAPTER TWO

RUBBLE MERCHANTS, SLATEHEADS AND OTHERS

Wales, 1987

Cigarette butts, crumpled beer cans, the Captain's been on the sofa for weeks. The carpet's still damp under stocking feet since the pipes burst in the winter. No gas, no fifties for the leccy meter, no window in the front door, hardly any food in the cupboard and no one's washed up for a month. But there's thirty bottles of spirits in the kitchen. Sell some of them and we'll have some dosh. It's daft having all those bottles of evidence in here though. The house is dark and smells of sweat and breath and mould. A muffled cough comes from upstairs. I creep up there for the bog. The door to Carlos's room is lying on the floor. That's it, I remember, Gwion kicked it in last night to make him go and sort Karen out who had put a bottle through the front door window and was making a scene in the street. The broken glass crunches under my All Stars as I step outside. The sun's been up for ages and pricks hot needles into my eyes. Spring's doing its thing now and the Snowdon railway whistles good morning. Its sulphur smell catches my nose. I'm uneasy on my feet down the steep hill of Rallt Goch. I spit as I turn into Goodman Street and ruffle my hair. That wakes me up a bit. The kids in the park slide and swing with their young mums. There's the Professor. He makes me shiver as he stops and watches the children through the mesh fence. All those things you hear are only rumour though. You've not to forget that around here.

I grind the gravel of the pavement under my shoes. It feels real – more real than anything that happened last night. In Pete's Eats the tea's too hot for my lips. I hunch quietly and watch the others through the steam. There's the Fly, bent over his plate. He's called that because he sometimes throws his food up and then eats it again. But I don't think he'll do that this morning. The Lobster looks as though he's had a long night. I try and avoid the Lobster, all red and shiny, short in his long robbing coat. He'll get anything for you, dead cheap. Give him your order in the café and he comes back half an hour later with the goods. Pulled two ice axes out yesterday and dropped them on the table. They say he's the most well endowed man in the village. I rub my eyes and try and push the hideous image out of my mind. The juke box is playing Jimmi Hendrix too loud and the smell of burnt liver makes me gag.

"Number twelve. Fried egg and beans."

"Yeah, that's me."

Women, aged before they should have, sag at the next table and push Embassy Regals into their mouths, tired of it all. Their husbands are in the betting office. They'll meet up at the chippy and chatter in a high pitch Creole of Welsh and English. Dafydd Chips, the second biggest boy in the village, will scoop their deep fried offerings into newspaper packets for them to rush home with up the steep side of Llanber'. Meeta comes in. Looking happy, she snaps her tobacco tin down on the table top. I have to hang on her words at this hour to decode her Swiss accent and she entrances me with tales of Bolivian jails and Indian mystics. I gaze outside and imagine distant places.

Rain is spitting onto the glass now. Looks like another slate day. The slate's best when it's showery, it dries in minutes. It's where it's all been happening of late, why I came here. I saw a picture of a moustachioed, muscley guy manteling these tiny edges, trying to put both feet next to his hands, grinding his nose into the purple rock, and not a runner in sight. Now I'm living with him, Carlos they call him because of his Spanish waiter looks, and Gwion. They're letting me doss there till I find a place of my own. No luck yet though, and I've been there six months. We did have an ace place before but we got kicked out after we got caught with a pin in the meter.

I asked Carlos about the photo and he told me he'd fallen off just after it was shot and went sixty foot. When I got here the slate scene was already big. The days when the mysterious Rainbow Slab was spoken about in hushed voices, a top secret location, were near since gone. The falls you could take off the hard slate routes were already legendary and I wanted to take one. I didn't have to wait long before I was emulating Redhead and Carlos by falling eighty feet off a new route I was trying, drunk on the Rainbow. When I came to a stop, four feet off the ground with my nine ripped nuts stacked on the rope at my waist and Gwion higher up the crag than I was, I was content, and later bruised. I need to buy some chalk.

The sky is sagging and dark now and the village seems to be resonating at a low frequency. The Lard (the biggest boy in the village)'s new van is throbbing to house tunes and he's sat inside his shell suit on double yellows, menacing. Last week he knocked Manic Ben over, right there in the street, in front of everyone. I don't return his stare. I must take care not to tread in dog shit on the pavement. There's Tatan on the other side of the street, "Hi, Tat." He looks ghastly. The other week on the way back from a day trip to Dublin, lashed up, the lads ripped his clothes off him and threw them overboard into the Irish Sea. He's always the brunt of their jokes, but they love him really. When he showed up at customs starkers, and the officials had to kit him out with a too small pair of nylon football shorts, they all had a good laugh. Climbers in yellow and pink tights and ripped jumpers are in the street, some live here, some are visiting. They pace around like peacocks, too colourful for a dark Welsh village. The old quarry men don't know what to make of them. The young locals react against them. I got pushed around in the street after hours a couple of times, but Gwion's a good man to know. He's a local himself, one of the few who hasn't gone the other way and doesn't want anything to do with the mountains. He's our mediator. He let the guys know I was OK and now I can drink a pint with the same blokes who hated me before. Outsiders aren't always accepted here, especially big-time climbers with inflated egos. I've become the same, wary of newcomers, safe in our group.

Some try too hard to be accepted. One guy, the Weird Head we called him, who appeared for a while, said he'd base jumped the Troll Wall. He just wanted to fit in, that was all. When Bobby confronted him and told him that we knew he hadn't, he broke down and sobbed. There's a lot of crazy people here, people who can't sit still. The place is like a magnet, and for some there's this perceived pressure to be crazy too. The ones that try too hard don't seem to last long, they disappear. This old slate mining village has many good people. It just seems unavoidable that it should make winners and losers.

There's a distant brass band and a voice from a tannoy. It's carnival day. I'll run up the hill and wake the guys and head across to Vivian or up to The Lost World maybe. "Yahoo, guys. Who wants to climb?" Gwion's psyched. Carlos isn't moving – he's turned nocturnal, stays in his room all day reading horror stories. Gwion apologises for hitting me last night (I was only trying to stop him from slashing his wrists on the broken glass) and then we're back out on the street. The carnival floats by, children in outfits with paint all over them looking self-conscious and, at the head of it all, this year's carnival queen. Graham Sis they call him, a fat man, very effeminate in his long red halter-neck. He drifts by waving in his lipstick, his dream come true. The village is heaving now and we hurry across the fields toward the big holes.

In the quarry they're all there; new routes going up all the time. Things getting repeated and talked about. The Captain's having a tormegamite experience on something loose as hell, sweeping as he goes. The Dawes is trying a horizontal double dyno with his tongue sticking out the side of his mouth. There's JR creeping up the rock, thinking about genitalia. Nicky is psyching up for her ninety foot leap into the steel black water of the pool and Skeletor is wrapping his vast ape index around the purple rock. The Giant Redwood is on a rope, trundling blocks to uncover a modern classic. Harms the Stickman prances up the Rainbow looking unhealthy (how can he do this on his diet of chip butties and Newcastle Brown?). The Horn pops in and flexes his tattooed biceps on Colossus Wall. Moose is soloing like a maniac 'cos his girlfriend's left him and Bobby's bouncing around like a thing on a spring. And there's the Tick, recording all these antics through the lens and turning them into history. Uncle Alan watches from the bridge and reminisces about the thirties, when he was blasting and pulling the slate out of there. He warns us of the dangers, the giant rock falls, but he's glad to see the quarry alive again. It's why Llanberis exists and why it had prospered for a hundred years, until the sixties, when it shut down and all the men had to look elsewhere. That's why, now, so many shops are boarded up around here. But this is a real village, with real struggles, not tarted up, making concessions for the tourists.

There'll be teams out on the island today, it'll be baking out there. I feel like I'm missing out teetering around in this man-made scar, and for a moment I want to be above the sea, brushing lichen off crimps with my finger tips, searching for ways through uncharted territory, studied by seals. But you can't be two places at once and it could be worse. I could have a job. Big G and the Waddy will be out there with car inner-tube knee pads on, bar-ring their way across some incomprehensible ceiling with sea-reflected sunshine dancing on their backs in a dark cavern. Pengo and Manuel could be taking a trip to the moon on the Yellow Wall and the Crook will have invented new jargon with which to describe an obscure nook or cranny which will be the scene of an even more obscurely named new route. Tombs the mathematician could be with him. "No money, no job, no girlfriend. Might as well be dead," he had said. Ben and Marion will still be on Red Walls, moving in and out of the quartz, smooth and solid after all these years. And there'll be Craig, making his name in a splash of colour as the sun sinks into a receding tide. Up in the mountains Cloggy is turning gold and Mr Dixon will be up there doing his own thing on the cathedral of rock.

So as hands tire and blood sugar levels drop in the twilight, the climbers home back to Llanberis, to eat badly and rush for last orders. In the Padarn they're all drinking – the farmers, the girls from the chemist and the Co-op, the hairdressers and the builders, the walkers and the climbers. That builder I've seen doing one-arm pull-ups on a door frame at a party and laughing at the supposed climbers who couldn't get near it. And there's big Tommy forcing his weight against the bar, as if trying to stop it toppling over, as he sinks his pints. Gabwt's standing on a chair shouting "*Hash for cash*" with his Nunchakas in his hands, terrifying those who don't know him, as merrymakers sneak out to the Broccoli Garden for some extra stimulation. That's Dewi playing pool. He killed the vicar with the end of a snapped off pool cue that looked very much like the one he's holding now. Once he was beating Bobby at a game when Bobby remarked without thinking, "Bloodyhell, Dewi, you're a killer with a pool cue!" We all stepped back and waited for the explosion, but he mustn't have heard 'cos he just missed the black and sat down. Those climbers over there are standing cool and not talking about routes and moves, even though they want to. I ask Johnny for the numbers on some route or other up the Pass. "Three, five, two, eight, one," he says and makes me feel about this small. But me, Carlos and Gwion are buzzing. We downed a load of our spirits before coming in 'cos we haven't any cash to buy drinks. Those Giros only seem to last a day or so and then you're skint for a fortnight until you post your next slip in. Tonight's dinner was a rotting cauliflower that we got from the Co-op for 10p, boiled up with five strands of pasta and a stock cube which we found in the bottom of the cupboard. We called it cauliflower surprise. But Carlos has usually got some scam or petty crime worked out to keep us in food and other stuff. Never mind. Tonight people will be queueing to buy vodka and gin and tomorrow we can eat full sets in Pete's. As last orders is screamed out Kenny the Turk erupts in a fury and starts spinning a cast iron table around his head. The crowd sweeps backwards in a wave and tries to paste itself to the nicotine-stained walls of the room. The guy who has fallen out of his wheelchair in the crush pulls out a baseball bat and lashes out at anybody who tries to help him. For a moment things are completely out of control until Ash the barman, five ten and thin as a rake, gets in there and calms the Middle-Eastern stand-up comic's temper. Just another night in the Pad really.

Out in the street drunks mumble to themselves, dossers look for dosses and the partiers want to know where 'the scene' is. So it's off to some terraced house under an orange street lamp to try and prolong the day, wishing sleep would never have to come. The house is throbbing with the beat and those inside are giggling and dancing and you can tell, by the look in their eyes, that some people will be up all night. But if you eat those 'shrooms you won't get to Gogarth tomorrow, you'll sit around and waste your day away. Next to some hot knives on the stove we swap our stories of bricking it miles out, or talk of the moves on some slate horror and how you should try it like this or like that next time. But some of the others are bored by your keenness and wish you would shut up and you suddenly feel self-conscious as the herbs take effect. You realise you've overdone it and are incapable of speech, and the girl you've wanted to work up the courage to ask is talking with that other guy. So you leave for home without saying your goodnights, tripping over your own feet as you head down the hill. In the dark house you get into your pit, lie on your back and drift off, your head swimming, dreaming about tomorrow.

CHAPTER THREE

LOST IN THE BROCCOLI GARDEN

It was a vile day and the gigantic breakers from the Irish sea were surging halfway
up the 400-foot wall, drenching the cliff top with spray. I came away with vivid
impressions of dripping, disintegrating granite set at a thought-provoking angle.

— Tom Patey commenting on Gogarth's Red Walls,
Climbers' Club Journal, 1966

It was in 1986 that the hard climbers returned to Gogarth, and in that year
an insular band of the young and not-so-young subjected the 'Mother of all
rock' to a bombardment of frightening and characterful new routes. That
same year my intense relationship with the Red Walls began.

There are two Red Walls, a left one and a right one. High, vertiginous,
wedge-shaped sheets of ancient quartzite, separated by a knife-edge
promontory. The oldest rock in Britain some say. The right-hand wall
became public property in 1966 when its first ascent went out on television, live. The show was called *Cliffhangers* and involved the likes of Joe
Brown, Ian McNaught-Davis, Royal Robbins and Tom Patey. This wall is a
contorted and sensuously confusing place to be. Parallel shallow dykes of
sandy, horned grovelling nearly always lead the climber into a cul-de-sac
and the shape of the wall is perspectively deceiving, luring you over the
edge when you stop at the tourist viewpoint.

The left-hand wall is different. A crimson headboard to the sea bed. From
a distance the upper two-thirds appear featureless and ill at ease atop the
lower third, a warped and undercut wave of a soft grey chalky substance.
To be on the wall is to be on a vertical desert of pocketed rock, and as a
desert, seething with hidden life. Sea slaters and springtails disperse in all

directions from behind the odd loose hold and the face is also host to some huge spiders (likened to my prematurely aged digits). Rare flora also abounds; round comfortable cushions of green cling to the wall which is also one of the few haunts of the Mad Sea Broccoli.

I'd only been to Gogarth once before, when I'd waltzed up Positron, stopping occasionally to gaze into the exposure. I'd laughed and shook my head in disbelief all the way. Then, looking for an enjoyable climb to finish the day on, Gwion Hughes and I rapped into the Red Walls for the first time. After being puked on by an ugly ball of fluff, we crouched at the bottom of the route Mein Kampf. Uninspiringly, the first pitch looked quite horrific, but looks can be deceiving. They weren't. It was a loose and awful climb to the belay ledge and then it was my turn to puke through a mixture of the smell and the terror. We escaped up the wall's namesake and vowed never to return. That night in the Padarn, over calming beers, one of the older guys revealed to us that Mein Kampf hadn't been repeated after seven years. So that was it, we were back there the next day, climbing a little direct variation too. For me it was love at second sight.

When sprawled out in comfort on the belay ledge of Left-Hand Red Wall it's hard to miss the hanging flake of Schittlegruber[1]. I was gobsmacked to learn that no one had climbed that flake so I rapped in and inspected it. I found an overhanging scoop with only a meagre scattering of holds leading up to the jagged shield of the flake. The scoop looked hard and difficult to protect and, once again, looks weren't deceiving. The climb, with Nick Harms, went OK, I was taking well to this type of climbing, and the line came to be one of the classic hard routes of the island. It was repeated quickly, for Gogarth, by Yorkshire men Dave Green and Clive Davis who likened it to Gordale Scar's Mossdale Trip, a famous tottering pile of limestone. I wondered whether this was complimentary or not.

The wall drew me further in, to the central sweep right of the Heart of Gold. Rappeling down and discovering continuous lines of pockets and seams, it was like unwrapping a surprise parcel. And once I'd torn it open it was just the gift I'd been waiting for. In 280 feet I managed to find one peg placement, a poor downward-pointing knife-blade, which would have to serve as a belay. With Moose (Mike Thomas) I descended to the foot of the route. I set off on a tramline of sandy pockets in the grey wave. The first protection came after fifty feet of overhanging pocket-picking, taking care not to snap off the brittle edges. It was a briefcase-sized block detached on five sides and attached on its smallest end. Once looped it had to be

---

1 A pun on Schicklgruber – Hitler's family name.

laybacked and manteled. The bloated bodies of the Monster Alien Spiders wait for prey at the roof. I pull by and gain a foot-cramping rest on a hanging porcelain slab a little higher. I arrange a clutch of shallow protection in the blind seams in front of my face and begin what looks like three body-lengths of wicked dink-pulling. I gained height in convulsions. Classical music I'd heard in some car advertisement droned through my brain. I stopped being scared and, after an age of schizophrenic debate, I convinced myself that I could not fall off. I then began to look at myself rather than the rock. It was as though my body climbed while I gazed on … Peg. Stop. A threadbare stance in the middle of this Broccoli Garden.

I wasn't experiencing the anticipated satisfaction of completing such a frightening pitch. It was the numbness. And it was also that I was hanging on a tied off knife-blade with one small foot-hold. There were some tiny slots that would take RPs, there and here, but I'd used all four of mine on the pitch below. "Please don't fall off, Moose," I shouted down, but not too loudly so as not to worry him about the state of the belay. He didn't come off and we filled every imagined nut placement optimism could provide. Expecting the next pitch to be OK, I tried to send the Moose up it, but every time an RP popped out of the belay and we dropped another heart-stopping inch, our nervous disorders got worse. After a valiant attempt he refused. I led up and, quivering, pulled off the boulder problem, a slap for a tiny edge a bodylength above a nut in a wobbly block. I flopped over the rim trounced, with the buzz of an arsonist (I remembered the burning moors). Sitting on top and trying to calm down with ice-creams, we wondered if the runners or the belay would have held what would have been a long free fall. I attempted to question why I went for those moves when I could have backed off, reversed down, but no one answered. (Did I ever pause to ponder as the hospital curtains turned to yellow?)

A murky September day. The sea mist, the diffused flashing of the South Stack lighthouse. The distant subterranean boom of the North Stack foghorn. A melancholy mood. The dull lapping of the waves reverberates around the huge Gothic archway at the very base of the wall. Having just failed an on-sight attempt on the shale corner at the back of the arch, which we dubbed Television Set Groove, I passed two limp rope-ends to Johnny (Dawes). Silently he tied in and set off up the actual arête of the arch. I dodged the falling blocks for over an hour. To us the impact of the rocks made loud crashes but the fog would eat up any sound we made, swallow our cries for help. Did anyone know we were down here? Then a large part of the arête came off and I instinctively locked off the brake plate, waiting for the exploding gear placements. He screamed and began to fall, I saw it, but then he caught hold of the rock again and continued upwards, up the grey wave. After swinging around a short roof and pulling off more quartz rockery blocks, Johnny found a Friend belay in a wide crack. The crack went up to an apex and then back down to the lip of a giant roof further to the right. I struggled up the arête and approached the belay.

Johnny stared at me with an expressionless face. Something was wrong. It took a while to place it, and then I sniffed. It was the smell, the smell of fresh soil coming from inside the crack. We looked at each other still in silence. The crack formed one side of a bus-sized block which had recently slipped. The block was the roof. It wasn't supported from below, only from above by, perhaps, some kind of vacuum suction. Johnny's only belay was constructed of three shifting Friends in the crack. With hardly a word I set off on the next unprotected traverse pitch. I edged sideways with loose spikes for my hands and dinnerplates for my feet, right on the lip, which kept snapping off. I glanced back at Johnny, just a loop of slack rope between us. If I fell would the centrifugal force be enough to bring the stance down? My head begins to swim with fear so I concentrate on the mosaic of bubbles and ridges just beyond the end of my nose and keep on blindly feeling to my right. Eight feet from the corner now where the promontory meets the wall and the loneliness begins to shake me. Boom, flash, boom, flash go the other inhabitants of Gogarth. The fulmars and guillemots seem strangely quiet. After a seeming eternity on one small muscle-cramping foothold, Gwion and Trevor appeared on the ramp. They broke the cathedral-like atmosphere with their chatting and laughter and this cheered me across to the last jump move into the corner. One, two, three … No, I can't. Yes, you can. I can't. *You can.* An internal pantomime raged in my head. One, two, three … Yes, gotcha! I clung onto the grass tufts of the slabby side of the promontory. It was all over. Come to Mother, we like to think, stood as a monument to on-sight climbing for five more months, before the roof collapsed of its own accord.

The next month I was back again, this time with Trevor Hodgson. I stole a fine direct on the second pitch of Heart of Gold and followed Carlos, as he was then known, up a short, hard direct start to Cannibal. But these were only to be fillers in before a new episode began.

In my search for unclimbed rock I began to visualise an almost imperceptible line between Heart of Gold and The Enchanted Broccoli Garden. It was a line marked by its lack of flakes, cracks and corners and would follow small edges and pockets from one tiny seam to the next. The first pitch had a small roof to be surmounted and the holds were hidden under wet tufts of grass. I climbed, ice axe in hand, cleaning as I traversed the initial overhang.

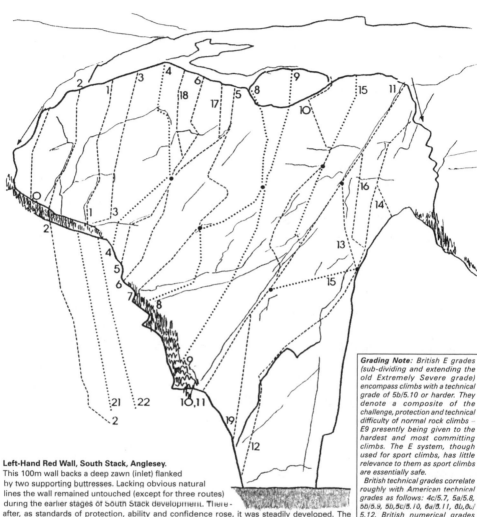

Grading Note: *British E grades (sub-dividing and extending the old Extremely Severe grade) encompass climbs with a technical grade of 5b/5.10 or harder. They denote a composite of the challenge, protection and technical difficulty of normal rock climbs – E9 presently being given to the hardest and most committing climbs. The E system, though used for sport climbs, has little relevance to them as sport climbs are essentially safe.*

British technical grades correlate roughly with American technical grades as follows: 4c/5.7, 5a/5.8, 5b/5.9, 5b,5c/5.10, 6a/5.11, 6b,6c/5.12. British numerical grades bear no relationship to French rock and sport grades which grew out of alpinism – French technical 6 being about British 5a/b.

Left-Hand Red Wall, South Stack, Anglesey.
This 100m wall backs a deep zawn (inlet) flanked by two supporting buttresses. Lacking obvious natural lines the wall remained untouched (except for three routes) during the earlier stages of South Stack development. Thereafter, as standards of protection, ability and confidence rose, it was steadily developed. The compact rock offers only sparse natural protection yet, apart from the odd piton, the use of fixed protection has been carefully avoided. Because of this, fine, challenging climbs were discovered by each generation of activists and Red Wall Left is now seen as one of Britain's key cliffs for demanding rock (i.e not 'sport') climbs.

0   **Vena Cava**
1   **Auricle** 1967 HVS/4c Joe Brown, Brian Fuller, (Mo Anthoine).
2   **Alligator** 1978 E1 Al Evans, Paul Williams, Jim Moran, Ben Wintringham.
3   **Cannibal** 1978 E4/5c Jim Moran, Al Evans, Paul Williams, Ben Wintringham.
4   **Schittlegruber** 1986 E6/6b Paul Prichard, Nick Harms.
5   **Left-Hand Red Wall** 1967/76 (FFA) E3/5c Joe Brown, Pete Crew (AL,2pts); Henry Barber and party (free).
6   **Mein Kampf** 1979 E5/6a Jim Moran, Dave Cuthbertson, Paul Williams, P. Aubrey.
7   **Heart of Gold** 1978 E5/6a Mick Fowler, (Stevie Haston), Phill Thomas.
8   **The Super Calabrese** 1987 E8/6b Paul Pritchard, Bob Drury.
9   **Enchanted Broccoli Garden** 1986 E7/6b Paul Pritchard, Mike Thomas.
10 **Pagan** 1973 E4/5c Pat Littlejohn, Andy Houghton.

11 **Deygo** 1968/73 (FFA) E3/5c Tom Proctor, Geoff Birtles (5pts); Ron Fawcett, J. Heseltine (free).
12 **Come to Mother** 1986 E7/6a Johnny Dawes, Paul Pritchard.
13 **Infidel** 1978/78(FFA) E3/5c Ben Wintringham, Joe Brown, Marion Wintringham (2 pts); Gordon Tinnings and party (free).
14 **Anarchist** 1978 E1/5b Ben Wintringham, Jim Moran.
15 **Salem** 1987 E4/6a Paul Pritchard, Pete Johnstone.
16 **Outside the Asylum** 1988 E5/6a Paul Pritchard, Pete Johnstone.
17 **Ramilina** 1991 E6 Mike Turner, Louise Thomas.
18 **Howl the Trowel** 1991 E7 Mike Turner, Louise Thomas.
19 **Yarding Lard** 1996 E6 Mike Turner, Steve Hartland.
20 **Care in the Community** 1995 E5 Glenda Huxter, Howard Jones.
21 **Ceefax** 1986 HVS Paul Pritchard, Paul Barbier.
22 **Horn of Plenty** 1986 HVS Paul Pritchard, Gwion Hughes (solo).

Notes: The author's climbs marked with dotted lines; AL – alternate leads; FFA – first free ascents. Arrows show principal abseil descent points. Main climbs only are shown – variations and girdles are not marked. The main stances are marked ●

Two king spiders watched me place a peg. This time they made me feel good. I took a fall whilst leaping across the overhang. The peg moves but holds. The thought crosses my mind that the spiders have smiled and granted me one fall. Next time up brings the Heart of Gold stance, once rumoured to be iffy but now recognised as bombproof in comparison with its neighbour. Nick, my partner for the day, refused to follow me so we left. Four months later an exceptionally bitter January day found Gwion and me sliding back down to the belay to attempt the next two pitches. Pudding and debauchery weighed heavily on my stomach and conscience, as I contemplated the accumulation of Christmas calories. The middle pitch only took a few minutes because there was no gear to slow me down, just clip the belay and go for the layback. And there I was again at the dreaded Broccoli Belay. Silently, I sighed with relief when Gwion shouted over that he was bailing out.

It seemed to be becoming increasingly difficult to find rope-holders for my escapades, so I jumped at the chance when Bob Drury offered his services. It was the last day of January and on the first day of February the seasonal bird ban came into effect. The rock had trickles of water but it had to be today or not at all. We slid over the edge from a world of coach tours and ice-creams back into the tilted desert. Two opposite universes separated by a right-angle. At the hanging stance Bob was intent on clipping into the abseil rope but I threw it well out of his reach. I began to regret my decision as I repeatedly almost came off whilst attempting to rock over onto a slimy nipple. Three times I contrived to scrape back down barndoor laybacks to the minimal sanctuary of the Broccoli Belay and re-psych. I squeaked the inside edge of my left boot and climbed up to the nipple on my outside edge. That gave me just enough stick and I rocked over; the only consolation a Rock One in soft red rock. The face above is steep and carpeted. I brush the hairy lichen from the rock with my hand and it floats into my eye. There is no more protection. I begin to shake, then I go beyond shaking and once again my mind enters that realm of depersonalisation. I move away from the rock and come back with a crash at the end of all the difficulties, retching, about to puke. Sitting on top of this Super Calabrese, watching the clouds billowing out on the Irish Sea and, beyond, the Wicklow Mountains silhouetted by the setting sun, which then begins to play a trick on us and lifts the mountains so that they are floating on shimering stilts, I am numb and unaware of what I have done. It never really attained a relevance.

I climbed some more routes on the Red Walls, but the big lines had gone. There is something sad about a cliff becoming worked out – for me it's a sign to move on. But there were still a couple of blanks in the guidebook that I wanted to fill. At last I found a keen partner in Pete Johnstone and we took residence in South Stack bogs in the winter of '88. Over a couple of freezing days we climbed Outside the Asylum, because we were alone in an insane world, and Salem, named after a famous Welsh painting depicting worldly vanity – a woman comes into chapel late so that the congregation will notice her new shawl, and in the folds of the shawl is the face of the Devil. The folds and contortions of the rock reminded me of that shawl.

I don't often go back there now, but I do remember a daydream – of becoming entangled in one of those viscid webs, cocooned, to be excised as a Monster Alien Spider, to face my existence, shuffling silently, watching and soloing on that red wall.

CHAPTER FOUR

A PIECE OF DRIFTWOOD

Do you want to know why I didn't think about you on all those other climbs? When really I should have been laughing and joking about all the good times there were. Berating you for being such a fool. Or even wishing that we could still be huddled by the dirty fireplace, under a blanket, in that freezing house we shared through that winter. Rock 3 Terrace. I think we'll have to go back a little way. To a starting point, if you like. Perhaps I should begin with our first Scottish winter trip.

We hacked it up to Ambleside in your very knackered Mini to get Fluff. Do you remember? I could never drive and you always cursed me. After a night at the Charlotte Mason disco, in that barn, where we didn't cop off 'cos we were too scruffy and drunk, we switched to Fluff's knackered Ford Fiesta and hit the M6. We slept, the three of us, sat up in our seats like crash test dummies, fermenting in our pits, with snow settling on the windscreen. Next morning in the posh Aviemore café they frowned at us and wouldn't give us a top-up of hot water. Not the right kind of clientele. So we set off late to the Northern Corries and you led a route, which one I don't recall, that neither Fluff nor I could follow. You held us both on the rope and took the piss, as you liked to do. We maintained that it was only because you'd hacked off all the ice but, really, we knew.

Then we headed west, to Meagaidh – remind me where we slept. Smith's Gully was a breeze. You barely paused to put a screw in, you were always so confident (Fluff thought too confident), and you moaned about the party in front holding us up. Luckily, if you recall we didn't have a map and compass, the skies were clear and we slid like lunatics down toward the car park. Slotted back into the Fiesta, we boated round bends toward Glen Coe. On Raven's Direct you did it again, teetering up slabs on millimetre spikes of metal, almost doing the splits in the verglassed chimney on the top pitch. I felt like I was learning from you – but wait a minute, we were beginners together. I didn't reveal my impression. I took the piss out of you, too. But you didn't like that and you'd snap at me. When you came back and I'd drunk a bottle of your beer you got angry and didn't know how to react. After sulking and making me feel like I didn't care, you made me pay for it, and ever since I got the feeling you thought I didn't respect you. I did. We did. But if we'd shown it, you might have got big-headed. As it was you went for things as if tomorrow might not arrive, trying to prove to the world that you could do it. And afterwards trying to remain modest. Sometimes not even telling what you'd done. But you knew we'd find out. You might disagree, but anyway, do you remember what we climbed next? We soloed all those gullies on Aonach Dubh, but they were too easy and we got bored like only young blind men do. So we stopped below the summit and built a snow fertility symbol big enough to be seen from the Clachaig. Well, it made us laugh. You were the rudest person I ever knew.

On the Ben we did Point Five and The Curtain 'cos we'd seen them in *Cold Climbs*. It didn't matter if the ice was good or bad, you just went for it, and so did I. Well, compared to rock climbing these ice axe handles were like jugs. We didn't think about what kind of crud the picks were stuck in. And hell! we could hang on all day. Sliding down Number Five Gully they scowled at us as we flew past roped together and screaming. I came to a stop and you slid into me crampons first and made my leg bleed.

Driving back home, I don't need reminding. Between Glasgow and Carlisle, going fast, surrounded by thundering, spraying lorries, 'I've Got the Power' playing loud on the stereo combating the noise from the engine. And the windscreen blows out. We had no cash or any way of fixing it so we just kept going. It was night-time and blizzarding on the motorway and we got into our sleeping bags, Fluff with his feet poking out the bottom to work the pedals. And we had to wear mittens, balaclavas, and shades to keep the stinging snow out of our eyes. I don't know what the hitchhiker must have thought with his thumb out below the street lamp as we, like the PLO without a cause, imprinted against the windows, waved through the front of the car and shouted "No room, mate." We had to turn the music up even louder trying to get a ton out of the Fiesta pelting over Dunmail Raise. And when the doors sprang open we fell out into the street, unable to stand, we were so chilled. But we were pleased with ourselves. And now I'm glad that I made that trip with you.

And then, less hazy in our memory, there was Eigg. Mid-summer. We went to free the Sgurr, and to be fair you did lead a scary pitch (and I took another fall, flying with that block which squashed my thumb), but we soon gave up and decided to regress. We went mad like children. You showed off your public school athleticism in the inter-island soccer match, we laughed, drunk, as we rowed around in circles, on millpond morning water in our 'borrowed' rowing boat. You danced the fling with schoolgirls at the village hall ceilidh. The sun seemed to shine all night and we stripped and swam at 4 am – the night those islanders turned up on a tractor loaded with ale and we carried on, scared that it all might end soon. But the one picture that I keep with me, a photo in my mental pocket, is of you coming back across the little sandy bay pulling that trunk of silver driftwood behind you in a washed-up pram, coming out of the sun like a perfect recollection. We sat at a dining table made of sand and ate the finest food from the island post office. That driftwood, just like a wild horse's head, which you went to such lengths to hump across the island and onto the boat home, is now in George's house. He's the keeper and he cherishes it. And when any of us goes round there, we touch it and it transports us to Eigg and a time when we lost our heads.

Dingle, Ireland. George, Glenn and me were sat in Tom Long's bar when the phone rang, drinking Irish coffee.

"Its for you, Paul," says Liam, and I walk over.

"Hello ... Hi, Zoe ... What d'you mean?" I shook. "OK, I'll tell the others."

The room had changed when I looked up, grown bigger and the angles were wrong. She'd just told me you were dead. Soloing on Snowdon. I told the others and Liam poured us three stiff ones. And three more. Then Liam had the idea to take us out in his boat, to see the dolphin. He said that dolphins had been used as a kind of therapy for ill or sad people, and when it surfaced right by us and looked at us, the moment felt important. There was this creature, free in all this space. Like you now, maybe.

We danced all night like we were dancing for you and we laughed uncontrollably as we carried Glenn, me at his hands and George at his feet along the harbour in the morning sun. We leaned against a flagpole and joked about you, called you the lighthouse; Ed Stone – Eddy Stone Automatic – the lights flash but nobody's home. You'd have got grumpy if we'd said that to your face.

I didn't think about you because of a whole confusion of reasons. Little disagreements left unsaid, you being in on some of my most cherished memories (I fell in love on Eigg). But – the painful but – in you I saw mirrored some of my recklessness, and others'. It's what gets you up things, past those moments of pinpoint contact. Isn't it?

CHAPTER FIVE

ON THE BIG STONE

"It'll never go. Yer don't stand a cat in 'ell's chance," said the old-timer and Johnny and I ignored him, as we sat in Pete's looking at the photos of The Scoop in *Hard Rock*. Much to Johnny's bewilderment I'd never done a route in *Hard Rock*, so I was psyched up. Ken Wilson's photos looked terrifying, Doug Scott with EBs and jeans on, looking gripped with the rope being blown out horizontally behind him, and the big colour photo of the giant tilted corners in the evening sunlight with the climbers looking like tiny stick people under those black overhangs. And the words didn't add to the optimism – particularly the bit about "over-hanging bands of loose schist". I had spent my Giro and had no money. Pete had just given me a chip butty out of pity but I was depressed. I wanted to go but knew that I wouldn't be able to make it. Johnny said he was bored with us lot never having enough cash and offered to pay for me. So I grinned and with no time for negativity we jumped in the van and headed for Scotland. We got as far as Llandudno when I realised that in my eagerness, I had omitted to bring my rucksack.

The ride went quickly as driving with the Dawes always does. Up the M6 we motored with The B52's playing loud and the windscreen-wipers working hard to maintain some kind of visibility through the torrential rain.

In Glasgow we tried to get our friend Face into the van and sweep him off to the outer isles but he was having none of it. He had just got a job at the Hoover factory and couldn't risk getting sacked. He refused to take us to his local Motherwell pub 'cos he said that if Johnny opened his mouth with his posh southern accent we'd be beaten up straight away. Along Loch Lomond the Dawes actually got 'the Hovis' (as the silly, top-heavy van was affectionately known) onto two wheels as he went for a drastic overtaking manoeuvre. I think I upset him a little when, never having driven myself and failing to grasp the concept of road danger, I didn't get at all fazed. At Fort William we stopped to buy provisions – three big cabbages, a bottle of cold pressed olive oil, a bottle of white wine vinegar, a sack of petit pois and a packet of panty pads (excellent for sticking onto the rock and soaking up trickles onto the crux smear). We also bought Moskill, Repel, Attack and Jungle Formula. We couldn't fail. Before we left I rolled up a malt loaf into a big turd shape and laid it out on the aisle floor. It gave us a laugh watching the shoppers disgustedly steering their trolleys around the offending dollop. It was even funnier to see their faces as Johnny stooped down, picked it up and munched it.

I hadn't visited Skye since my mother brought me there as a small child but I remembered the shapes of the Red Cuillin, like velvet cushions, and the way the patches of light shifted across them west to east. And I remembered her smoking cigarettes and I being shocked (she never did that) to keep the midges away. I couldn't remember anything else, though. We gave a ride to an enormous musical hitchhiker, all the way from Canada, on her way to play at the Skye folk festival. We had to help her squeeze in through the side door and the Hovis listed badly all the way to Portree. As he drove, Johnny would glance at me occasionally and grin with a lurid expression on his face.

Waiting at the outpost of Uig for the Tarbert ferry, I managed to squirt a jet of Jungle Formula into my eye. The warning label said keep away from plastics and skin and my eye felt as though it were melting. Passers-by stopped and pointed at the scrawny youth moaning and trying to drown himself in a muddy puddle in the street whilst Johnny guffawed with sympathy. On the boat, and now nearing our objective, the rains began again but this was beginning to feel like a real adventure, the likes of which I had never been on. At Tarbert we cowered in doorways, hiding from the rain. The sky was so dark it felt like dusk, though it was only midday. After some enquiries we found a man, Big John Macleod, who would take us on his tractor to the start of the walk-in at Amhuinnsuidhe Castle. With our huge bags we rattled slowly along a bleak lochside, past a deserted whaling station and the most remote schoolhouse in Britain. We climbed down from the trailer dripping wet and shivering and handed Big John a tenner. Johnny and I struggled to glance sideways at each other through the horizontal rain when he informed us dourly that it was "clearing up". Sadly, on a later trip when we tried to hire Big John again we were told that he had succumbed to the 'island fever' and had taken a shotgun on himself.

During a lull in the tempest we began our walk-in. After what seemed like hours of sprinting and collapsing with a large rucksack on back and front and large cabbages in our hands (very good training) we reached a dam and, wrapping ourselves up in the tent fly, bivvied exhausted. We were awakened by rain on our cocoon. I poked my head out into the morning and to my horror discovered that it was a rain of midges and not just rain. We panicked which is the best thing to do in a midge attack and, shouldering our four packs, ran away. To help keep the rain off we made cabbage-leaf hats which one could munch when hunger took hold and, after a few hours of stumbling around, we (kind of) saw it.

The bottom half of the mighty Strone[2] looked like the underside of some great beer gut. A steep rock-strewn hillside led up to the cliff and where the two met there was a wide band of loose-looking shale. Water poured out of the cloud that kept the secrets of the upper part of the mountain. The waterfalls exploded into spray hundreds of feet in front of the overhanging wall. It was falling from the lip of the face and seemed to clarify the distorted perspective that the cliff presented. I tottered into the valley with the hillside on my back.

After pitching our tent in what was to become the biggest water puddle in the surrounding area, excited, we raced up to attempt the first pitch before it went dark. The rock was quite unsound and the ancient RURP for protection disconcerting. Johnny led and after some trouble clambered onto a small ledge belay. It had been hard and more than a little dangerous but we had made a start on a climb we had been dreaming of for a long time. Down below our unhygienic lifestyle and diet of salad and sheep shit wasn't doing much to keep our recently acquired streaming colds at bay. Then the midge paranoia began and we stayed awake half the night exterminating each invader as it forced its way through the tent zip. When the morning came the space between the inner and outer tent was thick with the evil little buggers. We were prisoners. To make our escape we first drenched ourselves in Jungle Formula, though we knew that they went crazy for the stuff (they like to lick it off before biting you), then we lit

---

2 Strone Ulladale, renamed Sron Ulladale by the O.S.

yards of mosquito coils and, quickly opening and shutting the airlock, hurled the pieces into the bell. After a while we could pull our stockings over our heads and make a run for it.

After forcing down a pan of glutinous gruel we headed back up the hillside to continue our adventure. The day was clearer and I shivered as I tilted my head back to see the whole height of the crag. It was easier to face away from the rock and look up at the face out above my head. Corners staggered up the overhang, slashes on a sheet of dark material. Could they be linked? Higher on the face one corner was soaking wet and water drizzled out of the bottom of it and we felt it like pinpricks, wet on our faces. I knew we'd never get up that. The next couple of pitches went more steadily, a short technical groove and a long beautiful corner. The rock was immaculate and we could find no placements for our ice screws which we had brought for the schist. We shouted and waved at two men fishing on Loch Ulladale, the only others we were to see that week. On returning to our dining cave that evening we were warmed to find two trout lying there. "Bugger vegetarianism, pass me the penknife."

With the ropes now fixed up to the huge wet corner we had hit an impasse. The way on looked downright offensive. There was so much slime oozing out of the cracks that it wasn't even worth trying. The only feasible alternative was a ridiculous-looking forty-foot groove/roof thing running out over the glen. I spent the day hanging in slings while Johnny aided and cleaned the first pitch of our alternative free route. Eventually, that tedious but necessary job done, we could slide back down for more cold salad. The next day Johnny's enthusiasm got him up the pitch quickly after some sequence difficulties at the start. The flying groove pitch got us to a lovely sofa of a belay ledge back on The Scoop – to where Doug Scott pendulumed on the first ascent. I wasted the rest of the day trying to follow the original line up a technical arête and over desperate bulges, the loch below my heels. That feeling grabbed me again. That same feeling as when I first went to the Verdon at sixteen. The space, the updraught, the freedom. This is why I go climbing. It's easy to lose sight when you get fuelled by ambition. With the updraught came the sound of ruffling feathers and the golden eagle was below my heels now. Like I could have stepped off onto its back and ridden away. I climbed to below that infamous bolt and came down. "It might go, but not this week."

Before zipping off down the, by now, very spacy abseils we scoped out the possibility of a traverse left from where we could perhaps get back up and right. Again we had no choice. Being just a couple of rock rats, we struggled with our jumars on the fixed lines and all the while the midges followed us up the cliff. We even took to climbing with burning mosquito coils tucked in our hats. They say that things as small as midges aren't capable of conscious thought. But these! They made secret plans of torment. There was method in their torture. It rained continuously but the Strone, overhanging more than a whole rope-length, kept us dry and always gave us new hope when our free passage was barred.

The leftwards traverse was a joy. A useless peg under a loose block led to strenuous slapping across a sloping shelf and a hanging blade belay. Johnny swung through and took us up an easier face pitch to a stance below the final capping roof. Oh dear, we sighed, it looked blank and impossible. But to the right the overhang was stepped with a slanting wall running through it. There appeared to be no protection but there was a smattering of pinches and small edges. It was my lead but I backed off after placing a titanium angle in a hole. In a situation like this, lonely and homesick and faced with a terrifying lead, Johnny could be counted on to dispense with caution and just be downright irresponsible. It would be quicker if he led and, not being too proud to realise this, I handed over the rope-ends. The mood had now become very sombre and few directions were vocalised as Johnny lurched across the overhang, pinching and struggling to keep his feet in contact with the lichenous rock. On the lip, pumping, he fiddled a slider into a little slot and slowly, quietly sat on it. The last gear, the angle, was at the back of the roof. As he fiddled with the gear on his harness the slider shifted. "Aaaah, don't rip, don't rip." Then, as he was futily trying to place a blade in a blank seam, the piece stripped and Johnny plummeted. He disappeared under a band of overhangs and began a long pendulum. I held the ropes tight and watched with horror as they slid along the sharp lip, spraying a cloud of nylon fluff into the air. As one rope snapped, the blade tinkled on the rocks 700 feet below. Johnny prusiked up and, silent and worried, we did the space abseil and tried to get our heads together.

After a solemn discussion we both agreed things were getting a little out of hand. Johnny was shaken up and felt unsure about going back up. All this fear to be stopped ten feet from easy ground. We had to come up with a plan. We were halfway through our last cabbage and our head colds were intensifying.

Early next day Johnny ran up to the top of the crag and began rappeling, with me below shouting directions – "Left a bit, right a bit." A brief peek was all he needed to see he was only a couple of moves from easy ground, so off we jumared excitedly, dropping all the fixed line behind us. Committed now, Johnny began the pitch, went for the run-out and wobbled up to the last Scoop belay. We both whooped with delight. I led through up to the last easy pitch on perfect gabbro and we had a summit

Sron Ulladale (Scoop Face), Harris, Outer Hebrides.
Free routes – dotted, remaining 'un-freed' sections of original aid routes – dashed.
● – stances on the author's routes. AL – alternate leads; VL – varied leads.

1   **Moskill Grooves** 1989 Ben Moon, Johnny Dawes, Paul
     Pritchard (VL) E6, 6b.
2   **The Scoop** 1987 Johnny Dawes, Paul Pritchard (AL)
     E6, 6b, (originally E7).
2a **The Scoop** 1969 (the remaining aided section of the
     original route) Doug Scott, Jeff Upton, Guy Lee, Mick
     Terry. A3/HVS 1 bolt.
3   **Knuckle Sandwich** 1987 Johnny Dawes, Paul Pritchard
     (AL) E7, 6c..

3a **Knucklehead** 1977 (the remaining aided section) Paul
     Lloyd, Terry King. A4.
4   **The Nose** 1972 Doug Scott, Guy Lee, Dennis Hennek.
     A5/HVS (the dotted section indicates part freed in
     1994 by Johnny Dawes at E7, 6b).
5   **The Chisel** (Gloaming Finish) 1989 Crispin Waddy,
     Drury, John Biddle 1989; Waddy, George Smith (AL)
     E7, 6b.
6   **Sidewinder** 1971 (general line – now eaten into by
     several of the new free routes though large sections
     originally went free). Doug Scott, Guy Lee A5/HVS.

roll-up with the last of our tobacco. After the descent we buried lots of our equipment under rocks as we began enthusiastically making plans for our return, when we would attempt the other unbelievable lines (on return we never managed to find our cache). We ran down to Amhuinnsuidhe where we gorged on food from the remote post office that was ten years past its sell-by date and used the phone at the grand castle to call up Big John for a rescue. In the castle the gillies and watchers told us about Gerrard Poncho, the Belgian business tycoon, who 'owned' Strone Ulladale and charged £200 per bullet to shoot a mighty stag. In my pride I thought "He doesn't own the Strone right now. We do. And the eagles."

When we wrote up our free ascent of the Scoop in the Nevisport book we postscripted it 'On-sight', which it was, apart from the last ten feet. We felt we had tried so hard for that climb that we were entitled to forget about our little indiscretion.

CHAPTER SIX

BHAGIRATHI DIARY

It is better to waste one's youth than to do nothing with it at all.

— Georges Courtline

July 10

Walked into Bob's new office this morning to find him peering through the curtains, spying on those in Pete's Eats across the street. He likes to know what's happening, who's about. When he senses my presence he swings round on his swivel chair and lowers his shades. "Hey, Aardvark." This is his 'affectionate' nickname for me. "We've had more arrivals." Bob jumped up and beckoned me to the giant mound of boxes dominating one side of the office. "Soya Dessert, ten cases! We won't have to buy food for ages." Bob has sent a draft letter to every food, equipment and cosmetic company in the country and the swag has been rolling in for days now: five cases of mushroom pâté, mountains of chocolate, muesli, noodles, a case of Golden Virginia tobacco, hundreds of tins. Things seem to be getting out of hand. Last week I even got to visit a peanut butter factory. Watching it all oozing out of that giant sphincter made me feel sickly and I had second thoughts about walking out with twelve gallons of the stuff.

July 15

The portaledges we've been making with Hugh Banner are coming on. We hired a local machinist to make the tent which looks like a wendy house with a plastic window in it. A £100 voucher came from the Co-op to help us with our trip which we promptly cashed in for hard liquor at Leo's supermarket.

July 20
Had a fund-raising slide show at the Heights which went a bit crazy. Some of the speakers got too drunk to work the projector or even to communicate with the audience. First prize in the raffle was Johnny's Skoda which we had to push down to the pub. At least it tempted lots of folk to come, the fact that first prize was a car. The first winner didn't want it after she saw it and neither did the second. It must have been the spray can graffiti all over it that put them off. We pulled out loads of tickets before we found someone who would tow it away. We had to give some of the straighter members of the audience their money back. One said it was the worst slide show she had ever seen but the hard core seemed to like it.

July 30
Got our cheque off the MEF for £800. I'm made up as I wasn't sure how well I'd done at the interview. I was weirded out, there at the RGS with all those faces looking at me, and when Hinkes asked me if I'd ever worn crampons before I wanted to say "Course I've frigging well worn crampons before," but I just had to play it cool and say yes. We'll show 'em.

August 8
Thirty tubs of pear and apple spread arrived. We've been busy on Joe Brown's sewing machine making holsters. I bragged to Joe about the Golden Virginia sponsorship and he just told me to "Give that up for a start. It's a mug's game."

August 12
Portaledge trouble. And only thirteen days to go. Bob went on the radio in the garden of the station and pretended to be on the summit of Snowdon. Johnny's obsessed with synergy and wants to make a ledge that will turn into a sledge or a glider. Climbing's falling by the wayside as we speed around the country collecting stuff.

August 16
Got pulled and fined on our way to get jabs at the Tropical Medicine Centre in Liverpool for doing ninety in a fifty. Bob's not happy as he's been banned for years anyway for under-age driving. The Heights want us to move the Skoda out of their car park.

August 18
A week to go and the damned portaledges still won't work right. Once you put the thing together it won't come apart again. Our expert engineers at HB are doing a great job though.

August 23
Packing turned into a Soya Dessert fight on the banks of the Menai Straits and we practised with our new Charlet Mosers on a telegraph pole in the garden. Getting up the pole was easy but getting down again was a bit trickier and resulted in some dangerous falls with brand new sharp spikes flailing around.

August 25
Last night is too much of a blur to remember. We overslept. Outside Bob's house this morning there were bodies everywhere, under cars, in the fields and on the side of the road. Like an invasion of colourful giant slugs. We piled into the Dwarf's van and got to Manchester late. Even after extensive repacking and jiggery pokery – I had my pockets loaded with pitons, screws and other potentially dangerous weapons – our bags were still too heavy and the man wanted a grand in excess baggage. We became incensed: "But we're the official Bhagirathi 3 expedition, supported by the BMC. Surely we can arrange something?" We did. The guy let us on and even allowed me to empty my pockets of iron into the hold. As we ran for the plane the passport controller thought we were a rock band; Dawes has a bald head with a single plait coming out of his forehead, I've got my usual Mohawk and Joe and Bobby are in bright clothes, shades and jewellery and are swaggering around like a pair of rock stars. Sat in Moscow airport now waiting for our delayed Aeroflot plane to Tashkent. Just saw the airport cops beat up a black guy for daring to complain about this gross food.

In the air now. What a take off. The whole thing shook violently and the baggage compartments sprang open, jettisoning the luggage onto the heads of the passengers. Someone started to scream and was reprimanded by one of the burly hostesses. Just been drinking vodka at the back with a team of Siberian workers who kept trying to force mouldy sausage on me.

August 27

Delhi. What is going on? This place is completely barmy. When you get off the plane it's like walking into a steam room. We almost collided with an elephant that had strayed onto the dual carriageway on the taxi ride into town. In a traffic jam a woman came over and held her baby to the window. It had a hole in its stomach showing its intestine. I didn't have any money to give and didn't know what to do. I wanted to take them to hospital but we don't know how this place works. It smells really bad here, there's flies everywhere and people with limbs missing. But there's colour, too, and action to make cities back home seem like big brother is watching us. I'm going out walking.

August 28

Went walking last night with Bobby, just soaking the place up, and ended up in these tiny pitch dark streets around Payer Ganj. We heard groans and piles of rags would shuffle about in the dirt, but it wasn't worrying. In some downtown area in Britain we would have certainly been mugged. Today we met Simon and the rest of the team and they took us to a 'café' for lunch. Well, it was a corrugated shack stood on top of an open sewer. The cook was filthy, with a running nose and smoking a *bedi* and he cleaned our plates with a brown rag that also served as his handkerchief. Simon smiled, he was obviously trying to psych us out. But it didn't work. We tucked into the *dahl* and *roti* and, in the sweltering heat, washed it all down with dusty glasses of tap water. Johnny complained that his glass was dirty and much to all our mirth the cook wiped it clean with his snot rag. Later we drank copious amounts of fruit juice with crushed ice at a street stall. I had read somewhere that ice was dangerous but Simon assured us it was OK. We also met our liaison officer who is a truly repulsive man. Hermunt is short and fat and his teeth are rotten and yellow and he chews betel nut constantly and spits the dark contents of his mouth to the side of the dining table. At dinner tonight he boasted about his caste and seemed angered when I was not impressed that he was a Brahmin. He snapped his fingers at the waiters and also shouted at them if they happened to bring the wrong dish out.

One other ridiculous event of the day involved Johnny. We were all hanging out in our hotel room, trying to cool down, and Dawes appears with these three Sikhs. He tells us that they've told him his future and his past and that it's changed his life. He said all he had to do was write his mother's name on a piece of paper, making sure the Sikhs who where all around him couldn't see, then hide it in his pocket, and they were capable of telling him his mother's name. Then they told him he would marry an air hostess. He was so impressed he gave them seventy quid which we worked out to be about six months' wages for a Delhi cab driver. We took the piss out of him mercilessly and joked that he might fall in love with one of the Aeroflot women. Johnny actually had the last laugh though as tonight Bob and I went our separate ways to buy some of the fabled Indian *charas* and each came back with match boxes full of incense!

August 30
Hired our own bus, loaded it up and headed for the Himalaya. We'd only been going a few hours when in the dark we came to a halt. Up ahead there was a crowd shouting and flames in the road. It looked like there was a body on fire but it was hard to see, and none of us was going to investigate. It turned out that some kids were pouring petrol over each other and torching themselves. Hermunt explained that they were unhappy because the government had, in an attempt at equal rights for all castes, given a large percentage of professional and civil service jobs to the lowest castes. The students who had studied long and hard were now out of jobs and this was their demonstration. I am amazed at the strength of their feeling. Students at home might do some banner-waving, but this is on another level. I've got so much to learn here.

August 31
Uttarkashi. Met our agents who are going to organise our cooks and porters. It's a pretty shifty outfit. Mr Buddi is small and weasely with piercing dark red eyes and the first thing he did when we got in his office was roll a joint under the desk with one hand. He insisted we all smoked some of it before doing business and then slowly turned to look at us all in turn and grinned. Occasionally he ordered the boy out to buy ten cups of hideously sweet tea. Bobby and Johnny could not control themselves and began giggling. Then came in Mr Rana, the brother of Mr Buddi. He was short and muscular and looked hard as nails and his eyes were even redder and darker. Bob and Johnny had to turn away and hide their faces, they had lost the plot. When we got to our hotel we tried to pack all our equipment into twenty-five kilo porter-loads but we ended up just sitting and staring at the floor. I tried to sleep but I couldn't and I kept looking at the curtain for what seemed like hours as it appeared to dance before me.

September 1
Got on the bus bound for Gangotri. At first it was OK but as we climbed into the Gangotri Gorge our driver got progressively more stoned. On the mud road we were dangerously close to the edge many times and we could look

down a thousand feet to the wrecks of other buses. We took comfort in the fact that Mr Rana wasn't driving, as he was swigging back the whisky also. After a tea stop we climbed back aboard and, to our horror, we found Mr Rana sat behind the wheel. He offered me the bottle and put his foot down. We lurched wildly round corners on the road cut out of a scree slope as he played chicken with the oncoming vehicles. He kept grinning at us and gesturing for us to roll one up as we sped along. We all partook just so there would be less for him but at each *chai* stop he seemed to find more. At one stop Mr Rana introduced us to a friend of his. The man was tall and evil-looking and was draped in gold jewellery. He wore the smartest clothes and showed us his gold teeth with a sly smile. We shook hands. Keeping his eyes on us, Mr Rana nodded towards him and then looked sternly at us. "Smuggler," he said, breaking into a grin. Johnny looked interested and asked him just what did he smuggle. But the man only grunted and stared at us. Bobby was busy across the road reaping wild marijuana which grows everywhere.

We booked into a medieval hotel with stone beds and no windows and after unloading all our kit went to explore the village. This is the last settlement on one of the most famous pilgrimages in the world, to the source of the Ganges. There are naked men with long dreadlocks huddled under boulders, women selling *pujas*, flowers and things for throwing into the raging brown river and hundreds of well dressed Indian pilgrims furiously eating *dahlbhat* with their fingers in the tiny dirty cafés. There are monks and yogis and colour everywhere. In the temple the pilgrims queue to kiss the stone *linga*, Shiva's penis, in the morning cold. Bobby and Johnny are both complaining of feeling ill.

September 2
Didn't get much sleep last night as Bob and Johnny kept crashing into each other in their desperate attempts to beat each other to the bog. All night they were puking and shitting. On the walk today Johnny shat in his new tie-dye trousers and a New Zealander had to carry his bag as we were all too tight to help out. We have hired loads of porters and they have come from Nepal to work their off season. They are a good bunch. Saw Bhagirathi 3 today and it's hard to believe that we'll be on it soon. I feel funny from the altitude already.

September 3
I feel lousy. I'm in an ashram at Bhojbasa and I've been sick all night. The others have all gone but Johnny's stayed with me. I'm itching too, like there's fleas in this bed. I'll be better tomorrow.

September 4
Still feel queasy but have to escape the food at this place. Will start walking soon.

September 9
God, I feel dreadful. I'm back in bleeding Bhojbasa. It's a bit of a long story and only now do I feel well enough to write it down; Johnny and I left this place a day after the others, thinking we'd be up at base camp in no time. Neither of us has ever been this high before, even base camp is higher than Mont Blanc. We passed Gamuk, the source of the Ganges, where it comes spewing out from beneath the Gangotri Glacier and had a last *chai* stop with the *babas*. Then we climbed up onto the glacier and traversed the left side, like we were told to do. We moved dead slow 'cos neither of us was feeling brilliant. We walked all day over endless rubble heaps until we had finished all our water. It started to go dark and the camp was nowhere in sight, so we had to admit it, we were lost. Johnny searched for water and prepared for us to bivvy, whilst I nursed a blinding headache. We had a few sips with gravel in it and went to sleep in the rocks. I had a pretty bad night and in the morning we realised that we had gone too low and that the camp should be just above us. I felt dreadful as we scrambled up a giant scree slope and then I saw Uttar Singh, our young cook, above us. He came running down, smiling, and helped Johnny with his bag! At camp Bob and Joe were relaxing in the sun. I had a brew with them and crawled straight into my tent.

I guess it must have been a couple of days later when Joe came into my tent and forced me to get up. He told me he wanted to do some tests. I had been puking and moaning endlessly. I crawled out before the panel of Bobby, Johnny and Joe, who had in his hands a copy of *Medicine for Mountaineers*. How many fingers am I holding up? they asked me. How many hands are you holding up? I asked them. Walk heel to toe for us, they said. And I fell over. They whispered amongst themselves and flicked through the pages of their book and then they casually informed me that I had cerebral oedema. If you don't get down straight away you'll die, they said. But I can't walk, said I. I'll carry you, offered Johnny. And that was it, back to the hell hole of Bhojbasa. It was going to be a long piggy-back for the Dawes, but as we descended I felt better all the time and after a few hours I was able to support myself. He stayed for a couple of days but then went back up to the others. I've been hanging out for a few days longer, eating *dahl* and gravel soup in the black hole and listening to the Butthole Surfers in my room. I occasionally go outside and sit by the Ganga and just stare up at the mountains. I've been to America and Mexico before, but here I feel a long way from home. Everything feels way out of my control. I'll be back on track tomorrow.

September 11

Walked up to BC alone and felt OK. Johnny was there on his own as Joe and Bob had decided to switch to the Scottish route. He seemed a bit dejected that the team had split so early on, but the guys, who are back down from their carry now, didn't know when I'd be better. JD and I will have a look at freeing the Spanish route.

There is a tense atmosphere up here. Joe says he's not that happy climbing with people who've never been mountaineering before and that's why he wants to go just with Bob on the easier route. Shivling is incredible in the moonlight. There are more stars here than I've ever seen – it's so clear, so high and no smog.

September 12

Load-carrying today along the mudflats, past leopard prints, and up a heinous hill we called the Triple Cromlecher. We dumped fifteen days' food under a huge boulder below the West Face. I'm glad we've decided not to try it. It looks possible but I got scared just looking at it. The wall consists of an El Capitan of freezing granite topped with a thousand feet of disintegrating shale. When the sun came round and started to loosen things up you could hear the rocks spinning through the air for ages before they hit the base. Back here at BC Bobby and Johnny had an argument over a game of chess. I couldn't understand the waste of breath. And later Johnny and Joe had an argument about onions. The team seems a bit stressed. Maybe it's Uttar Singh's badly tuned radio which transmits an incessant din from the confines of his tent. At dawn, when the woeful wailing starts up, it is greeted by groans and shouts from the other tents. In the end Bob burgled the poor lad's batteries.

September 14

More load-carrying. When we got back up to our cache we found all our food had been eaten and we don't know by what. Perhaps it's blue bears or leopards. It's spooky up there. Johnny had to make his own rucksack for load-hauling today as he'd left his sack up at the cache the first time up. When he tried to use one of the others' sacks it resulted in a real barny. I hate all this conflict and I don't know what the hell's going on in everyone's heads. Things would be a lot easier if everybody calmed down. Guess we'll have to carry more food up.

September 16
Snow. Tent. Killed a fly. Perhaps I'll die.

September 18
Cleared up. All going up for an attempt. Bleak atmosphere.

September 22
Back at BC. Didn't do very well. My arm is knackered. When we got to our cache more of our food had gone, this time from zipped up bags. But we saw the critters – choughs. Choughs that can unzip bags! We slept out on a rock and got snowed on. It was freezing. Had a dreadful breakfast of porridge and set off too late for the wall. As we waded up the snow slope the rocks already started falling from above. We did a few pitches on granite and were close to the tower on the Spanish Pillar when we heard a loud whirring. A rock came from nowhere to hit me in the arm and knock me down the slope. My ice axe shot off like a boomerang. At the time I thought it might be broken but I got some movement out of it. Must be just badly bruised. So that was our big Himalayan adventure over. We kicked our bags off and struggled down after them. Then we spent the whole night scrambling over moraines and traversing scree slopes which were like sand-dunes, no mean feat with one arm. Johnny was a real help. Got to camp at dawn. Bob and Joe had come down also. They had got higher than us but were stopped when Bob developed a suspected hernia whilst dragging their inordinately large haulbag. He seems to be OK now though, just a little groin strain. Guess we didn't 'show 'em'.

September 30
Joe left straight away, keen to escape from a bunch of young incompetents I suppose. Got a lot to learn about mountains. Bob left soon after, to meet his girlfriend and tour the south, and Johnny headed back to university at Norwich. Uttar Singh returned to Uttarkashi also. I came over to the others' camp below Shivling. Andy's been painting lots of pictures of Bhagirathi, it looks wild from over here. My arm's no better yet. Looking forward to our tour of the south and good food and tropical heat.

October 6
Helped carry stuff up to Shivling for Andy and Sean and saw an awesome unclimbed tower of rock on Meru's East Face. One day I'd like to come back to that. Freezing cold now that winter is coming.

October 10
The boys did Shivling. Said it was very cold and they've got frost nip as souvenirs. It was way below zero here at base camp, so God knows what it was like up there. This is the coolest place I've ever been and I reckon I'm keen to keep trying these mountains. But for now, *get me out of here.*

OUTSIDE THE ASYLUM

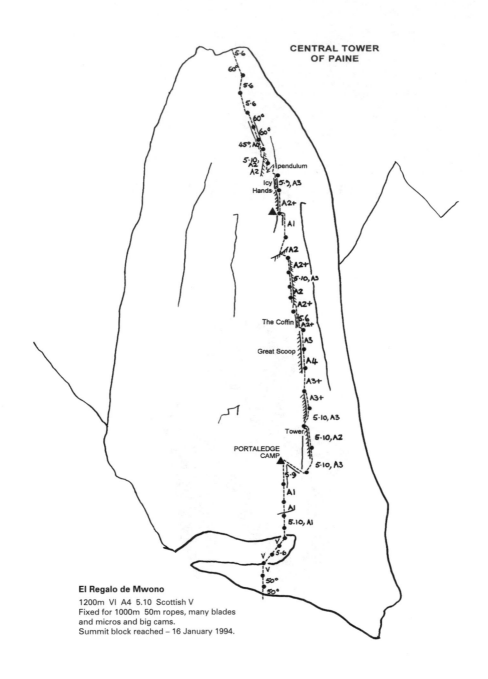

CHAPTER SEVEN

CENTRAL TOWER OF PAINE

5·6
60°
5·6
5·6
60°
60°
45°, A0
5·10, A2
A2
pendulum
Icy Hands 5·9, A3
A2+
A1
A2
A2+
5·10, A3
A2
A2+
The Coffin 5·6
A2+
A3
Great Scoop A4
A3+
A3+
5·10, A3
Tower 5·10, A2
PORTALEDGE CAMP 5·10, A3
5·9
A1
A1
5·10, A1
V
V 5·6
V
50°
50°

El Regalo de Mwono

1200m VI A4 5.10 Scottish V
Fixed for 1000m 50m ropes, many blades
and micros and big cams.
Summit block reached – 16 January 1994.

CENTRAL TOWER OF PAINE: EL REGALO DE MWONO

Imagination could scarcely paint a scene where humans have less
authority. The elemental forces prevail. In this desolation the wider
powers of nature despise control; as if to say "We are sovereign".
Here mankind does not look like the lord at all.

— Charles Darwin, Patagonia, 1834

A vertical sheet without horizons. Two dimensions. Up. Down.

Slide jumar up as far as it will go. Inhale. Weight foot loop. Pull with right
arm. Stand up straight. Exhale. Clink. Sit down in harness. Gasp. Look up.
No nearer. Slide jumar. Inhale. Weight foot. Pull. Stand. Exhale. Clink. Sit.
Gasp. Slide. Weight. Pull. Stand. Clink. Sit. Gasp. Slide. Weight. Pull. Stand.
Clink. Sit. Gasp. Slide. Clunk … Fraction point. A peg. Weight. Exhale.
Stand. Clink. Sit. Gasp. Darkness. Moving points of light. Remove top
jumar. Place above peg. Slide. Weight. Remove chest-jumar. Pull. Stand.
Replace above peg. Sit. Gasp. Repeat. Headtorch? No. Moon. Slide. Weight.
Pull. Stand. Clink. Sit. Gasp. Fear. Perpetuating other thoughts. Family?
Why didn't I? Slide. Weight. Pull. Stand. Clink. Sit. Gasp. Why did he shout
at me? Said he thought I was hypothermic. Hate. Sweat. Prickles. Slide.
Weight. Pull. Stand. Clink. Sit. Gasp. Repeat. Why doesn't she want me?
What more can I do to convince her? Wild swings of conviction. Should I
have gone to be a gold miner in Sierra Madre? The west coast of Ireland?
No. Look up. No nearer. Breathe. Above laughter. Chatting. Not alone.
Warmth. Food. Space. Still. A cavernous room. Spinning. Spiralling inside.
Thud thud thud. Giggling. Slide. Weight. Pull. Stand. Clink. Sit. Gasp.
Space. Nil comprehension. Emotion. Ever-changing. Sadness. Love. Anger.

A hundred questions. Why? Slide. Weight. Pull. Stand. Clink. Sit. Gasp. Pain. In hand. In shoulders. In arse. Sack pulling backwards. Gasp. Again. Sleep. Ambivalence. *Snap. Foos.* Guts rising. Screaming. Intensifying. Gasp … Awake. Inhale. Exhale. Repeat. Slide. Weight. Pull. Stand. Clink. Sit. Gasp. Repeat. Again. Lamp light. A rock crystal reflecting. A mirror. Repeat. Repeat.

My jumar hits a fraction point. A peg in the corner that I am in and I am shocked back into the night. It's 2 a.m. and we have been sliding up this line of ropes since the previous afternoon. The headlamp beam forms a mirror upon the wall. In this mirror I see the past, the present and appalling visions of the very near future. Below the rope fades limp into the darkness. Above it disappears, taut as a hawser, into the constellations of the southern night sky. Way below Sean follows. I know he's thinking about the state of the fixed line. In this dark it's impossible to see how much more damage our violent and unshakable companion, the wind, has made to our frail cords in the past five days of storm.

Five weeks earlier we had arrived in Chile joyful and unsuspecting, and with some glaring omissions in our badly packed equipment. Rattling down the country allowed time for our excitement to grow. Noel Craine and I were like the kids let loose, whilst Simon Yates and Sean Smith were the old hands at this world travel game. Hanneke seemed the most relaxed of us all. A Dutch woman, living in London, she had seen a fundraising slide-show of mine in the Heights, the Llanberis meeting place. Having always wanted to trek about Patagonia, Hanneke asked if she could come with us in the capacity of Sherpa, at which she was one of the stronger members of the team and very quickly became one of the gang. We went third-class on a train full of farmers lugging their crops from Santiago to Puerto Montt. Lucky as always, I found a canvas tent, which would be my home for a few months, left by the Boy Scouts under a seat.

We laughed and joked as the lush countryside floated by our window, until the train ground to a halt and we were faced with an ugly scene. Although we were only moving at twenty-five miles per hour, a *campesino* had stumbled onto the track right ahead of us and got under the wheels, somewhere in the Central Valley. Everyone got off the train to look as the drivers dragged out the badly mangled corpse. We were shocked by the reactions of our fellow travellers, "*Un boracho,*" they said, a drunk. Youths began breakdancing with ghettoblasters, a real party scene ensued and oldsters started passing around the *maté*, a potent stimulant drink made from herbs. It was only one year since Pinochet had been ousted and we wondered whether the people had been desensitised to death or just plain learned to live with it, and were now beginning to celebrate life again.

On the sixty-hour bus journey south across the Pampa, staring out of a dust-smeared window at the flat brown scrubland, it was easy to see how Southern Patagonia had become known as the uttermost part of the earth. Somewhere south of this monotony, over the horizon of this lens of barren soil, so level that in all directions you can make out the curvature of the world, so that it becomes simple to picture yourself on a great big ball, somewhere down there lay white and gold towers that even the most cloud-headed imagination could never dream up.

In Punta Arenas we tried to avoid sailors who wanted to drink with us. We were flattered to pose for photos and sign autographs for young women who didn't see many blond-haired guys on the Magellan Strait. "One kiss!" they shouted to us and we were happy to oblige. We drove past millions of burnt tree stumps, the legacy of the beef industry, *en route* to Puerto Natales where we did our supermarket dash and bought $700-worth of food and pots and pans. Noel bought a football, keen that we should keep fit playing soccer at camp. During our first game, and much to the gauchos' mirth, the ball punctured on a yucca plant.

When we arrived below the mountains we relaxed and partied with an American team who had been successful on the South Face of the Torre Centrale, and they gave us advice on big walling there. Eric, a huge, leglessly drunk wall veteran, told us to get up there and kick butt. We also partied with a local horseman who was to help us carry our kit to a camp high up in the beech forests. Pepe, a second-generation Croatian, and his family lived in tents in this grey and blue wilderness and, as they said themselves, had no use for the law. A man of great wisdom and few teeth, Pepe was to become our teacher in the customs and politics of Chile. He had seen many teams of climbers come and go. "Not many guys leave this place having made a summit," he had said as the carafe of wine diminished. Later in the evening he spoke of the other days, of how Patagonia, or Magellanes, had held out longest. But of how eventually the regime took hold. "The soldiers stood on my head and cut my hair with a knife. You were not allowed to grow your hair."

Walking behind Pepe's horses, Noel and I raced to turn each spur to see what would confront us next in the mysterious beech forest of the Vallee Ascensio. Black woodpeckers flocked on a bush and a pair of condors arced lines about the summit of Paine Chico. "It's like a zoo," pointed Noel when he saw a family of guanacos trotting by. The team thought it highly amusing to nickname me Nandu after the rhea-type birds which ran about the place. "Yeah, very funny, Simon."

At Campamento Torres we found two deserted cabins. Inside were fireplaces, black with years of use, well made botched furniture and plaques commemorating the great climbs, carved in their image with all the names scorched in below with red hot wire. In a side room off one of the cabins I found an oven made from a large square tin encased in stones and by its side a skillfully carved pizza shovel. There was even a wooden telephone which some homesick climber had lovingly whittled out, during some eternal infernal storm, to make a dream call home. I stocked the shelves of our new home, whilst Noel sorted out the wall gear with the impatience of a child – the weather was sunny and calm and we knew, from all we had heard, that it couldn't last. We each put up our tents about the tranquil microcosm under the forest canopy. The wind could blow all it wanted outside but in here it would be calm. Our retreat. We came to know it very well.

Three days after getting off the bus we loitered below the gigantic pepper pot of the Central Tower of Paine. I hadn't seen anything like this in my life, so overhanging for so far. It was like some kind of optical illusion, like it shouldn't be standing, like it should be falling on us. I stumbled backwards, off balance. The other three had all done big routes before. I was the only one who hadn't done this kind of thing. What if I let them them down? I was glad they trusted me. Noel and I were the best of friends and I knew he would always support me and help me through if I made a mess of things. I soaked up information and techniques from Simon and Sean. To me they were old hands, they seemed to know it all. They showed us how to make a snow cave and how to read the clouds, though the clouds didn't behave as they should. All four of us were indecisive and nervous and argued about where to climb. The other face, on the west of the mountain, was only half the height of the face we were looking at but it took the full brunt of the wind. I wanted to go for the biggest face. I have always thought big and gone for the most daring option and many times I have failed, but that's just the way it goes. The failures I have experienced far outshine the mediocre events of my life. After many hours of deliberation we stumbled upon a decision. The West Face was too far to walk and the East Face had *the* line.

We were the only climbers in the park. As we ferried our gear through wind and snow storms up the long talus slopes, we dined and slept in our own private forest. We now knew where we wanted to go. The steepest, smoothest and highest part of the East Face was split by a crack, but thin, too thin for fingers, for more than a kilometre. We were in awe but all agreed, over the sickly feeling this view caused, that we had to attempt this most aesthetic of lines.

Just as they had all told us, the weather was diabolical. At home that Patagonian veteran Rab Carrington shook his head and raised his eyebrows when I excitedly told him where we were off to. "What the hell d'ye want to go there for, lad?" he enquired. "It'll just piss down for two months!" We spent our first week burrowing up the initial 300-metre apron which was buried deep beneath unstable powder snow. Under the snow we sometimes found bolts and much later, when the snow cleared, we counted sixty on rock slabs of a VS standard. We were dismayed. Who would want to do such a thing? The snow made easy pitches difficult and insecure, and spindrift and wind-blown ice ensured that all time on the wall was very uncomfortable. It was slowly becoming obvious; we had come on holiday by mistake.

We clambered onto a sloping snowy ledge just below where the face got really steep and set up a multi-storey portaledge camp. We had been warned against using ledges in Patagonia due to the fierce winds. Indeed, a past expedition to the South Tower was aborted when a large chunk of ice fell right onto a portaledge camp, breaking an occupant's leg. But we were much too lazy to walk continually up and down the valley and, besides, the over-hangingness of the wall seemed to offer some protection. In fact, we hardly ever saw rockfall on this face and the huge pieces of ice seemed to fall horizontally with the south-westerly jetstream.

Simon pulled onto the ledge and scowled at me. "Don't just sit there, do something." I couldn't believe my ears. Who did he think he was. I had been leading all day and had set up this whole portaledge camp with Noel. Now I was taking a breather for a minute or two and he just arrives and tells me to get a move on! I felt like hitting him or telling him at least I could do hard rock climbs, but I just kept quiet and held a grudge for most of that climb on the Central Tower of Paine. I couldn't work it out. Back home in the pub he was always so relaxed and on our India tour he was easy-going when he asked me if I was into doing a big trip.

Andy Cave introduced me to him at the bar in a Harrogate hotel. I'd never been real mountaineering and I became transfixed that evening by his stories of faraway places; of Mark Miller getting beaten up by the taxi drivers in Rawalpindi because he'd spent his fare on a carpet, or the stories of tropical illness which Simon has had his share of (hepatitis, twice, or the mystery illness which, even after taking colon core samples, the doctors could never diagnose), or the many dealings on the streets of Delhi with

Indian con artists. I could smell the sweet hot air, though I'd never been there. This man interested me. Now on our first big wall together I started thinking I didn't know him at all. I didn't want to climb with him. What if he turned on me again? For the next few days I stayed partnered with Noel.

I never confronted him about that incident by the portaledges until recently when he asked me if I could give him a few impressions of the climb for the book he was writing. I told him how I felt at the time and he replied saying he thought I was hypothermic and he was worried about me. What I mistook for a needless attack was in fact Simon showing his care for me!

I remember, a couple of years ago, climbing on a big loose and vegetated sea cliff on the Lleyn peninsula, I asked Simon why he wandered around the world so and his answer made me reconsider my own plans to keep on travelling the globe. "Hey, I'm trying to move a lot less now," he said, looking searchingly out over the Irish Sea. "I'm only doing three or four trips a year now. I used to be on the move much more but that was because I was lost. It was something to do, there was nothing else for me. It became consumerism, like anything else, a list of places to be ticked off, and the experiences became flatter and flatter. I was searching for myself I guess." Then he turned and looked at me knowingly: "You'll do the same. You'll want to step out of the fast lane and find out where you are. You'll want a base and some stability." That was the first time I found myself resenting him and his arrogance. How could he possibly know what I want? At the time I felt like I was being lectured, told to settle down. But later, for me, layed up with injury and illness, some of what he said, not all, rang true.

The sloping ledge was the high point for a Spanish team from Murcia who had made two expeditions to get there. Three years earlier they had abandoned nine haulbags full of gear which we had seen from below and which did play some part in our choice of route. As we rummaged in the bags we felt some twinges of guilt but these were easily cast aside as we did have the backing of the powers that be: the park rangers had enquired if we would be able to get that rubbish down off the mountain. They had been eyeing it up for years and were wondering what kind of flash clothing they might get out of it. But bootymania soon turned to disappointment as we unpacked our vertical salvage. Inside the bags were mostly very bizarre items, including a barrel with hundreds of rotting batteries, huge flags with company logos on, a transistor radio and fluorescent strip lights. What was going on? We thought with this much gear it's no wonder they got no higher.

After a fitful night's sleep in our portavillage, comprised of a double and two single ledges, Noel and I set to work on the hundred-metre spire above the camp. Although too overhanging to hold snow, there was much ice in the cracks. Noel took the first of numerous falls when he unzipped a string of bashies on an aid pitch and dived ten metres. He accused me of dropping him, which I did, but I denied it vehemently. Well, I was cold and daydreaming to relieve the boredom ... And I did stop him, eventually. I ended that bout of activity by climbing an icefall in my flimsy rock slippers which froze my feet, so I packed them away not to be seen again.

The following day, while Simon and Sean worked hauling, the two 'crag rats' set about the Great Scoop, the formidable central feature of the line. Once again Noel tried to make swifter progress in slippers, but the intense cold forced him to lower off halfway up a pitch and don double boots. I then led on up a rotten choked up chimney. Halfway now and I was equalised on two tied off Lost Arrows, trying to arrange a blade. I heard the snapping of a hawser under tension, then more, and more. I knew what was happening, I'd been there before about thirty minutes ago, falling from the same spot. I bounced off the same ledge and landed on Noel again. He was disgruntled but still managing to smile, even though his belay was of the same wobbly pins as my placements. He seemed more upset that I had landed on him as he was rolling up his last tobacco. In time I reached another hanging stance on this great shield without the slightest foothold, a full rope-length above the last. I gobbed and it floated upwards like a spider's web on the breeze. If I followed that strange urge, the one that everybody gets when they look over the side of the Eiffel Tower, and untied, I wouldn't touch rock all the way to the glacier.

Christmas passed in an up and down succession of accelerating storms and retreats on ice-encrusted ropes. Weathering one forty-hour tempest in our constricted nylon tomb was to prove a particularly good insight into human relations when confronted by fear and poor personal hygiene. Through the maelstrom Noel shouted quotes from his book of quantum physics whilst I made long cigarettes from its pages. As we pondered Schrödinger's cat, the ledge began to fly like a kite and the seams of the tent began to split. Cooking in there was a dangerous procedure and used up valuable oxygen. Condensation poured down the walls and created a kind of soup under our sleeping mats. It was infinitely preferable to be the cook than the one who went outside to collect the snow. Noel passed two pots of snow in and perched on the end of the ledge desperately trying to relieve his inertia-induced constipation. I shouted at him to hurry as the spindrift was blowing in, and in his haste he fell off into the whiteout, stopped only after two metres by his slack tether. "Lord, I'm not cut out to be a big wall climber," he grumbled, and I giggled and shook my head as he hauled himself back into the ledge.

Then a day dawned calm and wondrous and two carbon-monoxide-poisoned figures jumared laboriously back to their high point. Noel began a huge overhanging corner with a stack of loose filing cabinets neatly slotted into the top of it. I was belaying directly below, in the path of any keyed in blocks he chose to unlock. To pass the blocks Noel first had to expand them with a pin, a delicate manoeuvre, and then aid up on micro nuts – I had nowhere to run. He would say to himself "I'm weightless. I have no mass." Using that meditation even the most dreadful RURP placement could be forced into offering some support. Two days of worry, daydreams, fear and mind games were consumed by that pitch. I ran out another pitch up a smooth overhanging shield and arrived at the base of the Coffin, one of the few features we had seen from the ground. Again it was getting late and we could see Sean and Simon starting the long jumar 600 metres or so below. It was time to switch shifts.

For three more days the corner went on through snow storms and past false horizons. Everyone was growing weary and the twenty-four-hour attention to knots, karabiners and each other's safety was becoming hard to sustain. Everyone had his close calls checked by his partner. But the view over the ridges into the surrounding valleys got better by the day; a little like climbing the oak in the back yard until you can see into the next-door garden.

Sean added to the collected air-miles when he stripped his gear out of an iced up chimney leading up to what was to become our top bivvy. The ground was so steep that it was an air-fall without danger. As the two 'mountaineers' prepared to spend the night up high, Noel and I rested at the portaledge camp, waiting nervously for a midnight start on the ropes. As we dossed and discussed relativity, we were startled by a twanging on the fixed ropes a few feet below our bed. This was weird because, aside from our friendly condors, we hadn't seen a soul in this valley for over a month. We heard heavy breathing and then saw a pair of gloves. Then we laughed when the face of our American friend, Steve Hayward, popped up with a cheesy grin. He'd jumared 350 metres to come and have a big wall party. We salivated as he unloaded wine, beer, chocolate, bean burritos, real cigarettes and mail from our base camp manager and coach, Hanneke.

The middle of the next morning we rejoined the other half of the team, careful not to boast too openly of our gluttony. We huddled together on a piss-stained snowy ledge a thousand metres above the glacier, with Simon leapfrogging bashies up a thin seam way above. We were pitifully low on 'biners and he had nowhere near enough to clip every piece. At last, forty metres out, Simon found a good Friend placement and weighted it confidently. *A scream* … With our heads flung back we saw his soaring buzzard form silhouetted against the grey frothing atmosphere. He bounced and somersaulted down the corner and hit a ledge just above our heads. He made a long whine with an occasional splutter. We attempted to lower him but the ropes had become fast in the crack. We glanced at each other, terrible thoughts flashing through our minds. A serious injury here, so far from help, could turn into a right epic. He came round and answered our worried pleas with, "The rope's stuck, I might have a broken arm. Give me a minute to sort this mess out." As he had fallen the rope had become sandwiched in a thin crack which made it impossible for us to lower him to us right away. He acted hard, Simon has survived some terrible ordeals in his past, and soon he had got himself down to the ledge. He rolled the arm at the shoulder and it seemed OK but he was shaking. He apologised for cocking up and, in that bad situation, I found respect for him and my grudge disappeared.

Noel re-led the pitch, throwing caution through the window (in Paine the wind is too strong), and I swung through into a vice of an overhanging chimney. Massive hands of water ice grew out of the granite at bizarre angles and I wriggled in the fingers like Fay Wray in the grasp of King Kong. I pulled myself free and it was like coming up for air – there was the summit block and lesser angled ground. We were euphoric. Screaming and yelping I sent Noel up the next pitch, a hidden crack which took a big swing to find. In darkness we fixed our haul line and lead rope and slid down to the bivvy with tidings of great joy. Dinner was cold porridge and rehydration salts.

The day dawned strangely; it was too warm and very windy. Water was dripping onto us. I stood up and my sleeping mat blew away and circumnavigated the summit block like some unpiloted flying carpet. We didn't pay too much attention to the ominous signs but within an hour a full thaw was upon us. We began by jumaring through a waterfall in the icy hands chimney. The nylon gardening jackets we had found in Noel's parents' garden shed had worked surprisingly well up until this point but were no match for this torrent of melting ice. Simon bravely led half a pitch but retreated, bitterly cold and in pain from the previous day's plummet. Sean, who had decided to go for the top in his canvas hiking shoes, now had frozen feet. Added to the fact that we had no food or gas, this fuelled our decision to bail out. We slid down a kilometre of wet, deteriorating rope, but our hearts slid further. Once on the ground there is an odd mixture of emotions. We didn't really want to go back up there, but we mouthed the words that we would. Did we try as hard as we could have done? Should we have moved faster on earlier days? All questions with no answers. We decided to escape.

We abandoned our base camp in the beech forest and ran the three hours to the roadhead, just making the last bus. Three more hours and we reached the fishing village of Puerto Natales. It was a depraved team of hill-billies that hit town. Starvation stares from behind scruffy beards and inane gruntings passing as language worried restaurant staff, who timidly placed endless plates of salmon in front of the savages, fearful of losing their hands. After a night in the bar, Sean and I visited the Mylodon Disco, a sound mountaineering decision. Reality became an obscure concept. A short while earlier we had been three pitches below the top of Torre Centrale, with all its sickly heights and violent winds. Now we were jumping to throbbing music below spinning lights of all colours. Velvet mylodons on the walls, senoritas, fluorescent liquids. Again I found myself screaming. We staggered out into the dawn and some local women helped us gain entry into another bar, though this one was obviously quite exclusive as it had no sign up and the door was locked. After a coded knock the door was answered by a blurred figure. Our friends ran away, I assume because they didn't want to be associated with us, but we gained entry. I remember a very spartan living room with crates of alcohol. I remember ordering beer and Sean collapsing. After rifling through Sean's pockets I had to admit to the blurred man that we couldn't pay, so I was forced to drag Sean back into the street. I wasted some time trying to pull him down the pavement but Sean Smith is a big man. There was only one course of action – I had to abandon him.

When I eventually located the hotel I found the others having breakfast. I was in a drunken panic and quite emotional. "You've got to come quickly. I've abandoned Sean." They ushered me out of the dining room because, they said, I was creating a scene and accompanied me to where I'd left him. When we reached the spot there was no sign of Sean, only a pile of vomit. Oh well! Sean's a big boy now. He could look after himself. When Sean did show up in the middle of the day he described how he had woken in a strange room and how he must have been carried in by the house-owner with whom he could not converse at all. That was just one in many instances of great Chilean hospitality that I have witnessed. And so, sated, we headed back to our mountain.

Noel was becoming increasingly agitated and we were not quite sure why. It soon came out that he had told his Oxford University bosses that he was going on a short holiday to Chile. He wanted to get back to his laboratory as quickly as possible. I stole his passport in an attempt to get him to stay but he played his trump card and pulled out a second passport. Damn! We were sad to see him go. He had done more than his share of the graft and he deserved another crack. True though, the near future looked bleak.

It had been a stressful time for all of us. The seemingly endless problems which the tower and the weather had put in our way made the relations between the team progressively more tense as time had gone on. For Simon it seemed an especially stressful period. Later he revealed that he had agreed to come on the trip almost out of habit, though truthfully he felt as though he had been on the move for too many years. What else could he have done, though? This was all he had ever done – gone from one trip to the next, around the world on some frantic whirligig of tropical cities, walk-ins and mountains. He had always ploughed forwards, blinkered, not wanting to look to either side for fear of seeing … a home … a woman … some stability … a bit of cash for a change, all the things he had previously seen as a trap, a part of the rat race. Maybe there was something in it; to live like other people and not like some perpetual wandering freak. After his fall and our frightening retreat in a furious storm he also chose not to go back up there. The state of the fixed ropes worried him and there was too much to live for now his decision had been made. Fair enough, I thought. There's no honour in dying, only image enhancement.

When my ascender hit the fraction point in the corner, I wearily removed the top clamp and replaced it on the rope above the peg. I raised my left leg in its foot loop and slid the clamp upward. With an effort I took my weight on one leg, unclipped the chest-clamp, stood up and replaced it above the peg. And so on and so forth.

At 9 a.m. Sean and I were together at the top of the ropes. The wind blew hard making shattering cracks, the likes of which we had never heard before, as the gusts exploded through the gendarmes above. At this moment the sky was blue. We had left our cabin in the forest a day earlier at 3.30 p.m. We had been moving continuously ever since. Over a few hours I led another long pitch with free bits, edging in plastic boots. I was tired of all this now and felt strangely detatched as I took risks above my gear. I was thinking about my father and his night club singing routines and how he liked to play the showman. But now I was the showman, as I took a large air-fall from a roof when I stripped a nut from a rock-ice sandwich. I had to wrestle with myself for control of my mind. There was no place for emotion here, only room for non-judgmental corrections and an awareness that an accident could have catastrophic consequences. Since the thaw the mountain had refrozen and the cracks had become choked in hard water ice. This made getting protection in time-consuming as every placement had to be chipped out. At the end of the pitch I arrived at a snowfield and above I could see old fixed ropes leading up toward the summit, not far away. This time, with the euphoria was a weary relief. But now it was certain. Just below, condors contoured the wall, shadows flitting from corner to face. Sean led through and after some mixed gullies and frozen frayed lines we wallowed onto the top. A different view! After twenty-one days on the wall we could at last look west. Lago Paine, La Fortaleza, El Escudo. The Fortress and the Shield. They appeared as hurriedly as they disappeared while the clouds shunted past with a fast-forward velocity. We were unable to stand and our eyes watered, from the wind rather than with tears of joy.

On the first abseil the ropes got stuck in some jumble of boulders so Sean had to reclimb the top pitch to release them. That wasted a lot of time and we didn't land on our top bivvy ledge until midnight. I immediately fell into slumber, whilst Sean kept waking me up with brews to rehydrate us. With the daylight came our early morning alarmstorm. The wind blew vertically, which made the already desperate task of cleaning a kilometre of rope, and dismantling a camp with only two people, even more desperate. Our ropes spiralled and twisted above us in the updraft, searching for crevices and flakes to hook onto and forcing us several times to cut them. In my haste I raced ahead a couple of pitches to a ledge and waited for Sean, but he didn't show up. After an age I leaned out and spotted him fighting with the ropes up in the foaming cloud. I shouted but my voice was ripped away from me. I could only wait. After an hour Sean slid to my side and went crazy. "I needed you up there and you just buggered off," he bawled in my face. "You were supposed to take the loose ends of the rope down to stop them blowing away. They fucked off round the corner and got stuck in a crack. It took me ages to free them." I apologised and felt ashamed. I had rushed things and put Sean at risk. Down to the base I tried extra hard to please, doing more than my fair share of the work. But we were focussed now on getting back to warmth and safety as we rappeled over the ice-coated rocks of the lower slabs. We descended the glacier in the night, front-pointing on twenty degree ice to avoid being swept away by the wind. And when we crept back into the forest in the early hours we didn't wake the others. In the morning Hanneke and Simon came into my tent and told me they were happy for us. I got tearful and went back to sleep. Celebrations didn't commence until a few days later.

Down in the meadow we were relaxing with Pepe and his family when we heard news of the imminent arrival of a Murcian expedition. There could

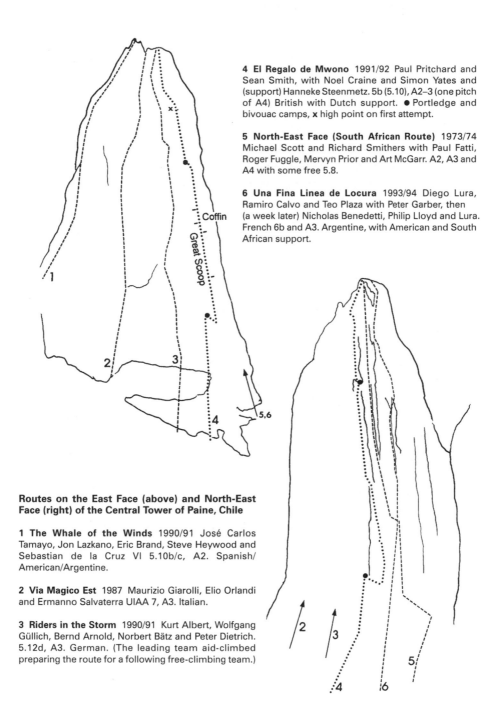

4 El Regalo de Mwono 1991/92 Paul Pritchard and Sean Smith, with Noel Craine and Simon Yates and (support) Hanneke Steenmetz. 5b (5.10), A2–3 (one pitch of A4) British with Dutch support. ● Portledge and bivouac camps, **x** high point on first attempt.

5 North-East Face (South African Route) 1973/74 Michael Scott and Richard Smithers with Paul Fatti, Roger Fuggle, Mervyn Prior and Art McGarr. A2, A3 and A4 with some free 5.8.

6 Una Fina Linea de Locura 1993/94 Diego Lura, Ramiro Calvo and Teo Plaza with Peter Garber, then (a week later) Nicholas Benedetti, Philip Lloyd and Lura. French 6b and A3. Argentine, with American and South African support.

Routes on the East Face (above) and North-East Face (right) of the Central Tower of Paine, Chile

1 The Whale of the Winds 1990/91 José Carlos Tamayo, Jon Lazkano, Eric Brand, Steve Heywood and Sebastian de la Cruz VI 5.10b/c, A2. Spanish/ American/Argentine.

2 Via Magico Est 1987 Maurizio Giarolli, Elio Orlandi and Ermanno Salvaterra UIAA 7, A3. Italian.

3 Riders in the Storm 1990/91 Kurt Albert, Wolfgang Güllich, Bernd Arnold, Norbert Bätz and Peter Dietrich. 5.12d, A3. German. (The leading team aid-climbed preparing the route for a following free-climbing team.)

only be one and they had probably already seen their clothes being modelled by the park rangers. We prepared for the confrontation by hiding when they arrived. Sean and I hid in a bush and watched the Murcians unpacking their two jeep-loads of gear and setting up camp. We began to get worried when they started to practise Kung Fu. What had they got in mind for us? The inevitable happened round at Pepe's shack one night and the four unhappy Spaniards came out of the darkness. It started with hand-shakes but soon degenerated into a shouting match. After informing us that their leader was so upset that he had had to go to hospital because his stomach ulcer was flaring up, they then demanded to look in our tents. Sean wasn't having any of this and, seemingly growing in the firelight, barred their way. What he wanted to know was why they used sixty bolts on the first 300 metres of easy slabs. A small scuffle broke out but no one was really willing to attack Tres Platos, the name by which the local gauchos knew Sean in respect of the inordinate amounts of food he could put away. We had nothing to give the Murcians. The few bits and bobs of clothing had been distributed among the gauchos and the rangers. The Spaniards left, hating us. Sean and I felt terribly guilty and left our ropes for the climbers, although they did seem to have arrived very well equipped. That was the last we saw of them, though we did hear that they went straight back home without attempting anything.

We named our climb El Regalo de Mwono, which means The Gift of Mwono, after the Tehuelche god who lives amongst those frozen steeples. The Tehuelche are gone now, wiped out by the settlers, many of them hunted down like animals. They chose never to set foot in the mountains for fear of inflaming the wrath of Mwono[3] but I knew that one of them, perhaps a young agile, dirty lad, dressed in a guanaco skin, would not have been able to suppress his curiosity and will have ventured forth and explored and hunted below the great cliffs. Though I doubt whether he will have considered climbing them. The gift was the climb, not the booty which caused so much bad feeling, and we felt honoured to be granted such a gift.

---

3 Mwono is misspelt as Mwoma in many journals and on the plaque in the Torres Hut.

CHAPTER EIGHT

PAINE NORTH TOWER:
EL CABALLO DE DIABLO

"Paul ... Paul ... Wake up. It's 3.30."

"Huh. Waaah?"

"It's 3.30. The stars are out and the pressure's still pretty high."

At that moment nothing matters. The whole world could go to hell. I wasn't bothered about climbing the North Tower of Paine anyway. My dream! There was somebody there I knew from back in Wales. Come back! Now see what he's made me do. I've lost the thread of my dream – if I look around every pebble-dashed corner, up and down the dark Welsh street, I might be able to find it again, under the orange cone of a street lamp in the mizzle. No. Gone.

"The Italians have already set off. Here, have some porridge."

The Italians! High pressure! The North Tower! My eyes sprang open and I wriggled out of my oily pit on the soil floor of the cabin. I looked at the altimeter, smiled, and forced cooling, pasty porridge down me with urgency, gagging.

"Don't they teach you how to make porridge in South Africa, Phil?"

Our footfalls upset a dark, cavernous forest and the rebounding stillness upsets me. It wasn't normal. A third day of high pressure and no wind. I had grown used to the wind and its rhythms and the creaking of the forest.

Now in the stillness I could hear whispers, whispers of conspiracy. I stepped up my pace to keep up with Phil. Yesterday we had relaxed in the sun on the edge of the forest, by the river where we could get a good view of the towers. A hot, calm day and we were too tired to go to our peak of ambition. The day before that we had climbed Planet Earth to Pisco Control, a silly name for what might one day become a classic climb on Paine Chico. We climbed that apron on friction and then hand cracks through leaning corners up the tower above, all free, and topped out at 10 p.m. The next morning, with our fingernails lifting from the dehydration, we couldn't get out of our pits. But today we had a dream. An unclimbed peak – just like Bonington and Whillans in '63, and again, twenty-nine years later, we were racing with Italians for the first ascent. But the Italians were an entertaining, noisy, laughing bunch whom we could never begrudge getting to the top first.

I struggled to keep up with Phil, a hard glob of porridge in my throat and my halogen pond of light bobbing, making shadows dodge behind trees or silently edge backwards. The Japanese camp was deserted. The cabins that the woodworking mountaineers had built whilst sitting out month-long storms were now like a ghost town on a spaghetti western movie set. I moved like an engine, too fast for my lungs, up the gully bed. The trees shrank until only knee-high and the world of towers opened out in the half-light. Only five or six of the shiniest stars still sparkled above Fortaleza and Escudo.

Phil stepped up the pace and I sweated. I couldn't curse him – like I couldn't envy him. His strength, his blond Viking looks, his educated conversation should have been all a pale, scrawny, uneducated Brit would want to be. But he was too big-hearted to inflame envy. And, of course, to be jealous of anything would be to make a mockery of this place we were in. Anyway, the deal was that he'd carry the heavier sack and I'd show him how it was done on the hard free pitches. You see, he'd seen my name in the magazines and was under the impression that I was some superstar free climber. And, what made it worse, I didn't try to side-step this compliment. I stood fast and preened my fame feathers. My free climbing renown, however misguidedly represented by the press, was my Dutch courage to tell confident anecdotes to, and teach techniques (from the safety of our cabin) to this, to me then, near perfect man. Over the weeks of waiting, for the rain to stop falling and the forest canopy to quieten down, I would feed him tales of dynos and long run-outs above RPs at Gogarth or other loose and overhanging British crags. Through the successive waves of storm there seemed little chance that I would have to prove my mettle – though I wanted to. And now we were panting with hot, wet backs and brows toward a pillar which draped down from its virgin summit like a princess's gown dragging on a boulder-strewn floor.

The Italians were above us in the snow gully and they had made good steps for us. Hanging back always pays. But they also had a head start on the wall – another Italian team had already attempted a line and had left ropes fixed on the face. I dragged my legs ever upwards, lagging further always behind Philip and I came across a tangled mound of wood with shreds of canvas skin hanging from its skeleton. I rooted around and found the words 'Paine Hilton' painted on what must have been a door – it was the original Whillans Box tent I had stumbled across almost three decades after its construction. As I collapsed at the base of the pillar our friends were already jumaring. We had chosen a route to the right, not the easiest way up but we thought the most beautiful – an enormous, bottom-heavy hourglass, it seemed now, of worm-holed and wind-finished granite, beginning as a slab and becoming overhanging 600 metres above.

To go extra fast we carried nothing except a litre of water, a small bag of dried fruit and our jackets in a small sack which the second would carry. We left our plastic boots at the base and set off sprinting. The deathly cold of the rock seeped into our hands and they too died, became brittle, so the skin would tear off the backs of white knuckles in gritty finger cracks. We arrive at a squeeze coffin, an empty iron maiden, leaning over us, nearly horizontal. The rope-ends are passed to me. I set off shaking with cold bones and, maybe, the fear of having to prove myself. But good gear appeared in the recess and, as I back and kneed out towards La Fortaleza, I mellowed and grinned, and hot joy poured to my guts. We both had that feeling as we climbed, the one that comes with those alpine starts, that you are still wrapped in your early morning dream. Not fully awake but a lifetime away from being asleep, feeling as though you know where the next hold or jam is without bothering to look up. We shouted across to Fabio, Mario and Danny. They were at the top of the ropes and had begun a nailing pitch. We were level now. The sun rolled out from behind the Central Tower and massaged our faces with its prickly radiation. We sat on a square ledge and nibbled stony dried peaches. Elephant-bum cracks and tower-block corners fell rapidly behind us and we moved well together. We could hear, but were blind to, the explosions of rock as El Escudo shed some shale over the edge of its table top, in a penny-pushing arcade game, at the other end of our arena. Over here, right now, our mountain seemed harmless, in a lighter shade of silence.

Then came a wall, the crux for sure, sheer and split by a thin crack. I moved towards it on edges, sandpaper-rough, and slotted my fingers, bony, into its positive locks. I keyed in a good hex just in time for the first strong breath to come, like a sigh, off the icecap, rustling nylon and flicking tapes. El Hielo Sur, as they call it here in Magellanes, exhales after holding its breath for three days. You expect it to come some time, it's just that now we had another contender in our race for the summit. I moved as quickly as my body, waking up to the strains of the day, would allow, placing my left slipper on the uptight edge of the crack and my right crushed into crystalline dishes which offered more stick, like squashing a beetle, than the steep wall around. My fingers slipped and skin ripped. Thick dark blood bubbled up on my chalky hand and I sucked at the iron taste. I knew I couldn't fall and I milked the crack for all it was worth, like some demented maid grappling with uncontrollable udders. Phil's shouts of encouragement echoed around the walls (or in my head) and I whooped out loud when I grabbed big jug holds. I got safe, hanging, and looked out west. Clouds poured like a mad scientist's experiment over the brims of our giant neighbours. But it couldn't be far now. We had to see how near we could push it. That shallow shame would always be there in the recesses of our minds if we bailed out now and the Italians climbed on. We egyptianed up wafer corners amidst ice-cream cornets for a few more comfortable lengths and arrived at a sundae ridge. We waded in our slippers, hugging the back of the mountain in defiance of the wind, which blew up the skirts of our jackets, up towards our summit …

A flash of red, and some gagged shouts. The team from Trento had just squeezed onto the top a couple of minutes before us. Oh well, *es la vida*! We hugged, shook and tried to smoke. Later, the photos made it look like we were gurning; the wind didn't show up on celluloid, only our struggles against it.

"Just like Bonington. A new tower!" shouted Fabio, happy in the storm.

They invited Philip and me to share their descent. It wasn't far down to the fixed lines, six rappels perhaps. We slinged a block, and with four ropes we dropped faster than the SAS, over roofs and down flat walls in the ventilation shaft updraught. At the lines we felt safe and began to clean them down, so the route would be left, unlike so many other Patagonian walls, free from never rotting threads, tempting future climbers to miss out the crux pitch and trust to unseen threadbare edges … Then the ropes were snagged by some unseen hand. The Italian trio were below us in the funnel-webbed corner. "Give it a good pull," I said, in what became the conclusion of the urgency with which we had started and spent our day. The way we led our lives.

One tug on this bell rope was all it took to peel away our good fortune and ring in the bad. The rope loosed and fell and in a baffled moment a house-brick rock followed. We pasted ourselves into the wall and screamed impotently *"Piedra!"* First Fabio took it on his head, then Mario clutched his leg and swung around silently. For a long moment all went still. It's funny how catastrophes don't always seem so catastrophic at the time. No flashing lights or flares shooting off, no screams of terror or fountains of blood – just an image, like a newspaper photo of an earthquake or something. You can choose to glance past it, move on to the crossword. It has all the impact you choose to attach to it. The two spinning in the wind could have been having a cheery chat or taking the piss out of us for, as so often happens, nearly wiping them out. But with rationale, the moment accelerated into urgency. No time for guilt just yet, we slid down to them as fast as friction would permit. Fabio giggled in his hysteresis and held up his broken helmet for our inspection. Mario moaned as we lowered him 300 metres. He was a big guy, mild-mannered and strong.

At the foot of the wall it was raining. Danny and Fabio, whose head, astonishingly, was not marked, eased off Mario's plastic boot to Italian cries of pain. Philip and I watched with sickly stomachs as the lower leg swung around wherever the boot did, like a second knee. Once the plastic shell was off and the bloody sock peeled back, Philip sighed to see the tibia thrusting up out of the front of his shin. When the leg was nudged a thick lump of dark blood would glop out and slither down his calf. He shook. We all did our bit; one put the emergency tent up, thoughtfully packed by Danny, others dressed the wound and splinted the leg with ski poles, and Fabio ran down to call a helicopter rescue. That would take him six hours if he kept moving. Philip, his chores done, held his head in his hands. I watched him silently torture himself with his very own herculean earth of guilt at what he had done.

But it was only your hand that pulled the rope down, Philip. I was the one who said to give it a good tug. I was the impatient one. And didn't Mario tell us he knew the risks that mountains offered, after all he'd climbed all over Paine. I just wish you were around to receive a postcard from him, cranking in Peru or on the Marmolada or the Cirque of the Unclimbables. I just wish you were here so we could go together and visit those mad Italians on their own mountains.

We slid down the slushy gully later to bring food and dry clothes up the following day. Philip was swifter than I and so I was alone again in the dark forest. Now the voices of the wood devils were clearer and I halted to hear what they were saying. *Troubletroubletrouble* the river muttered incessantly, and from the tree tops the leaves whispered *death … death* in rustly gusts. I cracked ribcage twigs and trod on skull boulders. From the mountains I could hear stranded climbers wailing from eternity. I had heard it all before in this magic forest but tonight it made my spine hunch up in protective spasms.

It should have been the sleep of the just but Philip couldn't calm himself. He had broken a man's leg and so now would not rest (only silently score patterns in the dark earth of the hut floor) to purge the guilt he felt. We abandoned our cosy cabin, with log fire and refried beans, before dawn and (I begrudgingly) returned through the cloud base. Midday we turned up with sleeping bags, mats, gas and nice food. Mario was loitering within his tent. In his own place with sticky drops of morphine. Danny's good humour was leaching into the wet snow. We waited ... Like long-suffering statues in a blustering, wet winter town centre, we stared out blankly into a prematurely induced twilight. Someone points out a useless fact.

"Can you hear that!"

"What?"

"Helicopter."

"Nah. It's a rock."

Boom. And a giant rumble comes from over by the Torre Centrale.

"It's a rock."

Minutes turn to hours turn to days turn to weeks turn to hours again in a didgeridoo wind of hypnosis.

Again. A pulse – to a different beat – very faint at first but getting nearer. Then like a flower-burst of hope over the ridge opposite a chopper surfaced, a tiny thing. The little black insect slalomed around the gusts as we shouted with clenched fists, thumping invisible tables – *"Yes"* and *"Yes"*, and encouraged Mario. The hovering bubble with the one big compound eye rocked violently, and once dropped like God had cut its string. It struggled to free itself of the fat cherubs' great puffs for a little longer and then, to our dismay, turned and fled. We pricked our ears and scanned the milky sky, searching for a sign, like four unholy prophets waiting for a door to open in the clouds through which might stampede the Devil's horses to our salvation.

You can hear it again. Rotor blades. This time coming from below. There it is, just above the glacier's bad complexion. Barely moving and wagging its tail. But it turns tail and deserts us. The wind punches us in mockery, left hook, upper cut. Below the belt. There would be no helicopter rescue – so we made our own plans. I picked my way down the thousand-metre snow gully, which was now a series of waterfalls, to guide up any rescuers, whilst Philip and Danny prepared to lower Mario. Back in the trees, the mosses and bark were electrified with colour, I sank up to my ankles in the shagpile floor.

I arrived at the cabin to find the Chilean army grazing through our supplies, leaning on their guns, all in fatigues and jack boots. They had come to help with the rescue and, initially, I was grateful. In my tent snored another soldier, clutching his rifle, just in case. I shook hands with Fabio who chattered, with wild eyes in a too fast mix of Castillano and his own tongue, about the roller-coaster helicopter ride he had survived. He had a mission in those eyes and was gone – followed by Dad's Army. I tried to keep the same pace but my plastics turned to concretes and I dry heaved. It was like someone had pulled the plug on my record – I ground into the ground and couldn't play anymore. I curled up and snoozed in a four-poster gully bed, pulling a leaf quilt around me. Just a few minutes. Just a few …

"Heh, huevon. Que pasa?"

I jump out of my dream, angry to have to leave Celia in that same orange lit, murky Welsh street. I was being shaken by Capitan Mainwaring and a group of journalists with big lenses who wondered if I was dead, they said. I guess I did look a sight. I don't bother to brush myself off, or explain my behaviour, before I regain my zombie strut in the tedious gully, followed by an excitable herd. I joined a growing team of helpers and spectators camped out at the base of the melting snow couloir. Fabio, Phil and Danny were lowering and sliding a green chrysalis, helped by other worker ants, Paula and Flavia, Italian partners. The Chilean army refused to go on the snow in their Doc Marten boots (which made the rescue much simpler), preferring to direct operations from below and throw the packing from our food around the moraine. I clambered up to my friends, sheepish for having been gone so long, though I had lost days somewhere. Phil turned and smiled briefly, but I didn't think he really noticed me in his strain of thought. I made myself useful by rolling a fag and sticking it in the pupa's mouth. It smiled back at me in a drunken sort of way. But it shouted out when we man- and woman-handled it down greasy crags, slipping and bumping. Fabio, who was close as a brother to Mario, took the rope at the head of his bound and bagged friend and dragged him through the snow, taking on himself as much weight as all us others would give. Like Gulliver and the Lilliputian ships, but he had a face full of agony. Mario was then passed onto the moraine shoreline from the ocean of snowy danger, into the hands of our fatigued lifeguards. Our corpse in a carpet suddenly became weightless as our testosterone-fueled friends eagerly proved their worth to us, passing him around like an antique Russian doll and marching off in a scrum, with a song, along the rubble ridge. Phil and I backed off while the others answered a hundred stupid questions, and the action was snapped that would be frozen on the front pages of tomorrow's nationals. But these badly shod paparazzi were an OK bunch, just a little out of their depth up here. But weren't we, also, doing a little more than mere paddling?

The Japanese camp welcomed us with open branches and spotlights from the beech leaf canopy. Tea was already brewing. The river played xylophone rhythms now and chatter and laughter competed with the mantra of the wind. Mummified Mario's ceremonious unwrapping was observed by an audience of faces all squeezed in. Flashguns flashed, questions were fired and notes were scribbled. Phil and I sat by the water, leant against an old mossy beech. He tossed pebbles into a green pool, occasionally glanced back at the throng.

"But it *was* a good route, Phil."

"Eh, it was." He threw another pebble with more force.

"What shall we call it?"

"El Caballo de Diablo." Slow, deliberate and well pronounced. A little girl we knew called Columba, Pepe the horsepacker's daughter, had shown us a Devil's coach horse one day and told us what it was called here in Chile.

"Sounds good." I meant it but perhaps, in my exhausted state, didn't show it. We both understood.

To our ears the familiar wind metamorphosed into the throb-throb of the little insect chopper and down it settled on the shingle beach, blowing on our faces. I got a lump in my throat. We all held Mario's hand before they slotted him into the black bubble to fly him off to Punta Arenas, eighty miles away. The insect lifted off and the trees leaned to let it through. They swayed back in to prevent a long goodbye and the sound was soon stolen back by the wind. We were left to mill around. It was late February and, for us, the end of the climbing season.

The Italians returned home to their jobs and tight families. Philip and I went to Argentina for more adventures before I went my own way on my nine-month wander of South America. Mario got an infection in his break but recovered within a year, so he could continue his work as a Dolomite ranger.

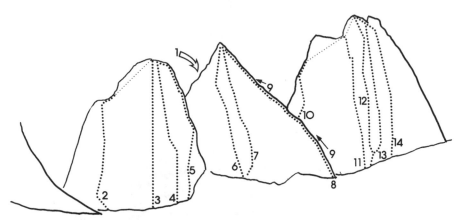

The North Tower (left and centre summits) and Central Tower of Paine (right) – North West Faces (Based on topos and reports in the American Alpine Journal with some changes).

1 **East Face (Kaweskars)** 1993 Anthoine Cayrol, Francois Bemard with Tierry Petitjean, Laurent Fabre, Hubert Giot.

2 **Armas y Rosas** 1993 Lorenzo Ortiz, Jose Chaverri.

3 **Adrenalina Vertical** 1992 Mario Manica, Fabio Leoni, Danny Zampiccoli.

4 **Suetra para Mañana** 1992 Carlo Besane, Nobert Riva, Mauricio Garota, Manuela Panzeri, Umberto Villota.

5 **South Buttress (El Caballo de Diablo)** 1992 Paul Pritchard, Philip Lloyd.

6 **Capachín Tórtola** 1993 Ramiro Calvo, Diego Luro, Teo Plaza.

7 **Ultima Esperanza** 1992 Michel Piola, Vincent Sprüngli.

8 **Corn Wall** 1993 Paul Pritchard, Celia Bull, Leigh McGinley.

9 **Via Bich (Monzino Route)** 1958 Jean Bich, Pierino Presson, Camillo Pelissier, Leonardo Carrel. (from Col)

10 **Central Tower, Original Route** 1963 Chris Bonington, Don Whillans with, in support, John Streetly, Vic Bray, Barrie Page, Ian Clough, Derek Walker. (from Col)

11 **Kanterarikez** 1991 Jon Lazkano, Kiki de Pablos plus, in support, Guillermo Banales.

12 **Wild, Wild West** 1990 Scott Cosgrove, Jay Smith.

13 **Via Defrancesco / Manica / Stedile** 1987 Fabrizio Defrancesco, Mario Manica, Fabio Stedile. 1987

14 **Via de las Mamas** 1992 (line on AAJ diagram but details not recorded).

CHAPTER NINE

JUST PASSING THROUGH

The *maté* gourd was passed my way again. I sucked it dry, the bitter taste convulsing the opening to my gullet. I was told it was good for me and, as I knew, the taste of anything good had to be acquired. The candle had a double in the black glass of the hut window. I shivered. It was a freezing night. Los Chicos played chequers and planned new routes for tomorrow. After three months in Chile I could hardly recognise their tongue as Castilian. The sound of *Metallica* came from the kitchen. They played their heavy metal all the time and they grew their hair long and wore leathers and beads. Here, somewhere in Argentina, a small pocket of teenagers mirrored other pockets of climbing subculture in the UK or America. They were living for the day and for the rock. And on the rock they were already experts, tutored by their, at twenty-one, elder statesman Sebastian de la Cruz. Sebas, spindly, nervous yet driven to the point of obsession, of Swiss descent, had climbed the giants of Patagonia at sixteen and los Chicos had followed, climbing Cerro Torre, FitzRoy and Torre Centrale sometimes by new routes. I was impressed by their ability and drive. It's more difficult to give it all up for climbing in this country. There is no welfare state and, with the Catholic church, religious values are stronger than in Britain. Las Chicas are stretching on the wooden floor in the candle light. They're into metal and rock too but seem a little less inclined to give up their career options totally. Gaby and Marcella study in nearby Bariloche and Fera works in the ski area in winter, teaching and guiding. Las Chicas and los Chicos seem to do everything together; climb together, eat together, party together and sleep together. They chatter incessantly and make plans for their next day.

I was dizzy. I needed air. *"Buenas Noches, Chicos y Chicas"*. I stumbled out of the *refugio* door into a night which was a long way from home. Frost pinpricked the exposed and unexpecting flesh of my face. It pinpricked the skin of the sky too and stark light shone in through the holes. This night was strangely two-dimensional. Scores of spires were silhouetted against starlight and crowded around like Klu Klux hoods. I liked *maté*. To look down on the lake was as to look up at the sky, creating the illusion of being suspended in the centre of a giant ball, dark, matt, but with millions of tiny holes. I buried my head in my pit and began to dream on the shore of the lake.

An almighty explosion.

I jumped bolt upright in shock. So did Phil.

"What was that?"

"I don't know. A meteorite perhaps."

"Yeah, right. G'night."

"G'night."

We awoke with the sun. The Klu Klux hoods were now bright shadowless spires. Five condors wheeled above the highest one, el Torre Principale. Over breakfast we pondered the mysteries of the night and decided that the next evening we would take more *maté*.

We shouldered our packs and went exploring. The mountains were further away than they appeared. We gazed at the panorama from above the forest canopy for these dwarf beech grew only to our nipples. Bluey chinchillas ran up and down the vertical walls. We arrived at the base of the Pyramidal and touched the rock. It was warm and rough to the touch. Unclimbed cracks were lined up side by side.

"Wow! This must be what it was like in Yosemite in the fifties."

The *vias normales* had perfect lines but new rock was the essence of climbing for us; throwing loose holds over the shoulder, feeling the exposed grains crush like sugar on footholds, no chalk ahead to show the way and no idea, apart from a contract which the eye has with the body, of whether you are capable of getting up a thing or not. I uncoiled the rope at the bottom of a hand crack which snaked up the wall and flared through a roof. The rock was deep red liver. The crack went, just, but intolerant. It meted out its punishment like Wackford Squeers, so that's what we named it. I had the bloody hands to prove it. From the summit we looked across to the Chilean Lake District and its volcanos; Osorno and Villarica, floating on a plate of cloud. On the Argentine side was Tronador, the Thunderer, that later claimed Teo's life in an unfair avalanche. Out east shimmered the brown Pampa and, nearer, the resort of San Carlos de Bariloche fitted snugly between the Andes and Lago Nahuel Huapi like some South American Interlaken. The tourists down there would be buying their ski passes and eating famous chocolate. Nazi war criminals who had escaped Europe after the war used to live there. Perhaps some still do. Nearer again los Chicos and las Chicas could be seen and heard laughing and ascending other spires. I felt then that Frey was another special place. A place where climbers lived who cared for it, and knew it well enough to say that the yellow rock was more brittle than the red, or that there are hidden holds inside that crack, or that the number of condors is on the up, that the boulder in the next valley gives good shelter, or at what time exactly does the sun shine on that face of the mountain. Simple shared knowledge. That which we have of our home rocks. And, for all their magnificence, this particular specialness is lacking in the more remote mountains of the Himalaya or amongst the Patagonian giants. Very few climbers live through all four seasons in those places.

"Las Malvinas son Argentinas. Las Malvinas son Argentinas."

That night the army arrived, a hundred of them with horses. They made a lot of noise and crapped a lot. I became the butt of all their Malvinas jokes and agreed, we shouldn't have sunk the *Belgrano*. But I came out on top after selling most of my gear to them. With that cash I could head on to Brazil and Bolivia. They had come to lay their yearly siege on Torre Principale and for days a khaki ant line was lashed to the tower which buckled under their enthusiasm and jollity. With the *maté* the nights became more feverish and the dreams more intense.

It was getting late in the season and a cold wind blew in from the icecap. Climbers were migrating. Phil, my transient South African friend, to the Atacama Desert and los Chicos, after evading national service, to Peru. Ramiro was the only one who had to have his dreads cut off and join up. They sat around the radio and listened to the lottery of numbers, each with their own army number, which they had been recently posted, clenched in their fists. *"Siete, dos, cinco, tres"* the officer's voice had said over the air waves and Ram's head dropped with his friends' hands on his shoulder. He wouldn't get to Alpamayo and Huascaran now. I took to soloing for a while.

In the shade it was cold but, if I turned to the sun, I felt its warm hand on my cheek. The 180-metre Torre Principale stood stark white above me. I was the only climber in the whole of Frey that day. I took my clothes off, it felt like the right thing to do, and put my boots on. Goose flesh prickled up on my body and I started to climb fast to keep warm. The first couple of pitches were easy but on the exposed off width of the third pitch the wind picked up. Though my genitals had shrunk dramatically, I couldn't help scraping them on the edge of the crack. Higher, a more sheltered steep corner began with a boulder problem which was luckily above a ledge. This led more easily up to the notch between the twin summits. I huddled up and shivered in the shade of that notch until I could linger no more. I tiptoed onto the summit block which leaned over a dark void and I crimped and edged, pecking at holds like a chaffinch toward where there was no more rock. The condors were near. This was their country. Now they were below me as they spiralled the tower. Their giant wings against the wind made the sound of an aircraft or sometimes, and not without surprise, the whoosh of a falling rock. As I climbed higher the rock fell away before me and I broke into a sort of vertical sprint. I manteled onto the top feeling like a chimpanzee, stooped, with my arms swinging low. I surveyed the now familiar world below and sensed something had come to an end. I opened the heavy summit tin and, after signing my name in the book and reading the soldiers' comments, I began to wonder how I was going to get down.

CHAPTER TEN

THE DOCTOR
AND THE WITCH

The dimensions of the room grow alternately larger then smaller. I can still remember my name, though I don't care to. Faces I think I know, faces I don't, come and peer over the edge of some invisible rim every minute or every age, I don't know. The bed is wet under my backside. I'm so hot I'm burning up. I itch. I want to sit up and ask these people what is going on.

"*Se parece peor, no.*"

"*Si. Vamos a buscar un doctor.*"

"*Es un buen idea pero hay unas brujas afuera en la calle.*"

What are these people talking about? Where am I? Hold on. I remember. It's becoming clearer.

I'm fighting through dense undergrowth. It's very hot and sticky. The wall isn't getting any nearer. Rat and Iñaki are up ahead and I am following with Kiko. Early morning and so hot already. This jungle climbing freaks me out, since getting stung by giant black bees in Rio. Every insect makes me flinch. They say there're hundreds of kinds of poisonous insects in the Amazon. There must be spiders all over these trees just waiting to drop on us. Big hairy tarantulas and black widows.

THE SLATE BOOM
North Wales climbing was revitalised by the developments in the Llanberis slate quarries in the early eighties. Many of the routes had long run-outs with marginal protection, calling for great skill, coolness and tenacity. These photos illustrate three of the finest slate climbs: **Rainbow of Recalcitrance** E6 6b on Rainbow Slab *(right)*; the author making the critical moves to reach the bolt and sling on **Raped by Affection** E7 6c *(left, top)* and leading the first ascent of **I Ran the Bath** E7 6c with Nick Harms belaying *(left, below)*. **Photos:** Iwan Jones *(right)* and Tony Kay.

THE ANGLESEY SEA CLIFFS

The slate boom was matched by an equally intense period of new routing on the North Wales sea cliffs, most notably on the Left-Hand Red Wall of South Stack *(above, top left)* and in Wen Zawn of Craig Gogarth *(above, right)*.

South Stack's Red Walls had been comprehensively developed, except for the blankest headwall in the Left-Hand Zawn. Here Pritchard's leads of **Enchanted Broccoli Garden** E7 6b *(first ascent photo – left, below)* and the very serious **The Super Calebrese** E8 6b, *(above, top left – a repeat showing the author leading the critical second pitch with Andy Popp belaying)* marked a distinct rise in wall standards in the area. **Photos:** Ben Winteringham *(above, left)*, Tony Kay – Pritchard Collection *(below, left)*.

On the overhanging back wall of Wen Zawn the Dawes/Smith creation **Conan the Librarian** E6 6b, captured the headlines in 1986. Paul Pritchard and Nick Dixon then added **The Unrideable Donkey** E7 6b, to the left of Conan *(above, right – with Pritchard on pitch 1)*. Later Pritchard nearly died here when he fell to the zawn bed from **Games Climbers Play**.   **Photo:** Tony Kay – Pritchard Collection.

SRON ULLADALE

The 200-metre overhanging end wall of Sron Ulladale on the Isle of Harris was first breached by Doug Scott's three aid climbs in 1969, 1971 and 1972. Paul Pritchard and Johnny Dawes forced the first free climb up the face in 1987 (**E7 6b** – based on the original line of **The Scoop**) and later added **Knuckle Sandwich** E7 6c and, with Ben Moon, **Moskill Grooves** E6 6b.

These climbs triggered a full scale assault on the cliff with over fourteen major new routes pioneered in the period up the late nineties (many found by Crispin Waddy and his friends), leaving Sron Ulladale, at the time, as one of the main venues for very hard on-sight traditional climbing in Europe. Sron Ulladale was most recently in the climbing news when Dave MacLeod and Tim Emmett climbed a new five pitch route – **The Usual Suspects** E9 7a – live on TV in August 2010.

Scenes during the 1987 first free ascent of **The Scoop** – the original route (1969) on the face. Johnny Dawes and Paul Pritchard enjoy a midge-free moment below the cliff *(below, right)*. The overhanging Scoop section is on the left. Pritchard leading the first pitch (6b) *(above, left)*, Dawes hanging out *(below, left)* and Dawes on the final Flying Groove (6th) pitch *(above, right)*.   **Photos:** Alun Hughes.

CENTRAL TOWER OF PAINE

Paul Pritchard, Noel Craine, Sean Smith and Simon Yates added a fifth climb on the East/North-East flank *(above, top right)* in 1991/92. These cliffs were first climbed in 1974 by the obvious diedre-line in the sunlit area. Three lines were then added to the face to the left *(see topo p81)*. The British team took a line up the right of the shadowy face, based on an impending diedre (the Great Scoop), followed by a chimney (the Coffin). Above these, at the 29th pitch, deteriorating conditions, plus food and fuel shortages forced a retreat from the face. Five days later, Smith and Pritchard, after a night of jumaring, pushed the route to the summit block. The pair managed to remove the bulk of the fixed equipment during their descent. The slab apron below the face was pointlessly equipped with over sixty bolts by Spanish climbers during an earlier attempt.

The Great Scoop proved the hardest part of the Paine climb. It had two long pitches, the first led by Pritchard, with a major fall, the second *(opposite, far left)* by Craine. "It had a stack of loose filing cabinets slotted into the top of it. I was belayed directly below, in the path of any keyed blocks he chose to unlock. To pass the blocks Noel first had to expand them with a pin, a delicate manoeuvre, and then aid up on micronuts. I had nowhere to run. He would say to himself, 'I'm weightless. I have no mass.' Using that meditation, even the most dreadful RURP placement could be forced into offering some support."

Opposite, below right: Simon Yates climbing up to the foot of the Coffin pitch using a crack in the wall of the approach groove (5.6, A2+). **Photos:** Sean Smith.

Above, top left: At the Portaledge Camp at Christmas — Yates abseiling. The climbing involved exploiting the short spells of good weather between the regular Patagonian storms, all from this rugged but serviceable hanging campsite. **Photo:** Sean Smith.

High on the face a pendulum gained a crack system which led to less steep terrain a few pitches below the summit. At this critical point *(above, bottom)* a major thaw soon had the rocks streaming with meltwater, forcing a return to the valley. After a morale-boosting session in the fleshpots of Puerto Natales Pritchard and Smith felt 'rejuvenated' enough to return *(top, centre)* to the mountain, jumar 1,000m to the high point, and tackle the final difficulties *(opposite, top right)*. After ten hours of climbing (including a fall) they finally gained the summit area but, with time pressing, did not climb the final icy seven-metre obelisk. **Photos:** Noel Craine *(bottom)* and Sean Smith.

MT ASGARD (Baffin Island)

Mt Asgard is a magnet to big-wall climbers, particularly the imposing western flank *(opposite, top left)*. In 1994 Simon Yates, Paul Pritchard, Noel Craine *(above, left top, L–R)*, Steve Quinlan and Keith Jones set up a boulder/snowhole camp on the glacier below North Peak's West Face.

The plan was to tackle the West Face without the use of bolts. But whereas the Paine Towers are riven with vertical cracks, the Baffin walls are ice-eroded and blanker. Americans who had attempted the Asgard walls believed that any future route would require bolting, or at least riveting, to link features and make progress.

Bad weather extended the schedule and Jones and Yates were compelled to leave for home. Luckily the Spaniard Jordi Tosas was able to team up with big-wall expert Quinlan to make up the foursome.

The line chosen had the most linking features, starting with an obvious series of flakes which led towards a corner system in the centre of the face. A long free pitch, then a section of aid, was followed by a pendulum to gain the Great Flake which Craine climbed free at 5.10 *(opposite, top right)*. On the wall above vague seams and incipient features (blank sections turned by pendulums or riveted), led to the central corner where a Portaledge camp was sited *(above, centre)*.

In the corner the aid difficulties unexpectedly increased *(above, right – Quinlan leading)* with brittle rock and shallow seams, climbed with copperheads and birdbeaks, giving two **A4** pitches. A pendulum gave access to Pitch 10 – **A2/A3** cracks *(opposite, below)*, which led to a skyhook and rivet traverse to gain access to the diorite vein.

After eleven days – climbing in the Arctic light, non-stop, day and night – the final seven pitches (5.8 – 5.10) brought all four climbers to the summit. *(above, left bottom, L–R: Tosas, Craine, Pritchard, Quinlan)*. They had kept the drilling (all by hand) to 36 rivets and 10 bolts. There followed a 16-abseil descent de-equipping the route of the fixed ropes and camping gear. **Photos:** Pritchard Collection.

TRANGO TOWER

Craine and Pritchard (part of an 8-person group) targeted a new route on the North Face in 1995 but, early on, Craine was injured in a crevasse fall. Pritchard teamed up with Adam Wainwright (on his first Himalayan season) to try the Slovene Route (5.10, A2 or 5.12b). After one attempt (to five pitches above the Shoulder) bad weather forced a retreat.

Above right: The upper tower from the Shoulder — the route takes the central apron to overhanging corners.   **Photo:** Bill Hatcher.
Left, top The team, L— R (back) Geraldine Westrup, Noel Craine, Kate Phillips, Adam Wainwright, Andy Cave, Capt. Jamal Mohammed; (front) Celia Bull, Donna Claridge, Ali Hussein Abadi, Paul Pritchard and Ismael Bondo.

A week of storms left the peaks encrusted with snow and ice. At the earliest moment they left the shoulder for a rapid lightweight summit push, only to find that every crack was choked with ice (*Left, centre* – Wainwright powering up one of the upper corners). The lightweight tactics gave problems with just one pair of rock shoes, one pair of boots, one axe and no crampons – between two. On the third day, in deteriorating conditions, with Pritchard having been hit by an ice block and showing signs of altitude sickness, Wainwright took over all leading and at 6.30 the pair reached the summit (*Left, below*) during a fierce wind. With all stances 'equipped' it took just two hours of urgent abseiling to regain the Shoulder!   **Photos:** Pritchard Collection.

"Hola, Paul. Hemos traido una Bruja. Te va a mejorarse."

What are they saying. Translate. They've brought … a witch … who will make me better. They have set a paraffin stove up by the bed and are boiling water. The old woman pulls some dead plants from her colourful bag and stuffs them into the pan.

"Aqui, bebe."

A witch! I've seen them out in the street, lined up selling llama foetuses and coca leaves. What's she giving me. No. I don't want it.

"Bebe, bebe!"

She's making me drink from the cup. Ahhh, it's revolting. GET THAT STUFF AWAY FROM ME. I nearly puke again but I've nothing left to give. The big woman with the bowler hat on disappears and I'm …

At the base of the wall now. We think we've found the start of the route. Salinas has a big North Face, twenty pitches they say. There's no cracks anywhere to be seen, all face, dead run-out apparently. Kiko and I go first. I lead in a still heat. It's easy to start with, just scrambling. Then it gets steeper and I have to think. I've brought some nuts but there's no place to slot them. The cloud forest opens out below us as we climb above the canopy. Kiko begins singing and I join in. We whoop and whistle at our friends below.

I'm on my hands and knees in a corridor. I think I wanted the bathroom, or have I already been? It was that dog, I know it. I was camping below Condoriri and that dreadlocked dog came and licked my pans in the night. For days previously I had shat by the same rock and every morning I would find my shit had been eaten. It was that dog, I know it. That dog gave it me. If I see it again I'll shove its balls down its throat, the dirty hound. I've got to get myself cleaned up. Got to get myself back to bed. I stagger into my room. My bed has a large brown stain on it. Outside the window I can hear the witches touting their wares and there's a brass band approaching. I pull off the sheet, throw it under the bed and climb back in. I want to go …

"Mum, I was just attacked by a group of boys. They shot at me with air rifles and chased me." I lied to her again and she took me out driving, looking for the yobs who would dare to threaten me. We drove up and down the lanes in our blue Datsun, scouring the countryside. It made me feel happier. Did you know that I lied to get attention? You were good to us, but with the family breaking up you had to work hard to build a new life for us. At the time I thought that you just had no time for us. She looks at me kindly and says I know.

But it's so hot here, and my head is pounding. Sweat is stinging my eyes.

The rock is steeper now and hot to the touch. There's never any gear, just a rusty old bolt every half rope-length that the local Brazilians had drilled. The pockets in the granite slope and my hands are sweaty. Watch me, Kiko, watch me. There are evil cactus and giant yucca growing out of the rock. If I fall I'll be impaled on these evil things. My fingers begin to slip. I don't want it to end like this. I want to …

Get better. To carry on with my South American adventure.

Who's this?

"Soy el doctor, Paul. Tu amigos mi dicen que no te sientes bien."

Damn right I don't feel well. He's asking me question after question and it's all blending into one. I wish someone would speak sweet English to me. He is going in and out of focus and talking with others. NO I DON'T WANT TO GO TO HOSPITAL. *No mi voy al hospital.* Get me in there and I'll never come out. He's pulled out a big syringe and is squirting liquid from the end of it. So cold. It's so cold. He's putting the needle in my arm now. I don't feel anything. Just the cold. I need to get to …

The top of the wall is a long way above and the clouds have come swirling all around us. This mist is wet and freezing cold. Should have brought more clothes than just this shirt. We are forced into a long leftwards traverse now by an overhang above our heads. There is no protection in sight. Our friend Sergiño, the capsicum farmer, who pointed us at this mountain, said this was the most difficult passage, 5.12b. That's a hard grade for these conditions. I cast a worried glance toward Kiko, my Argentinian friend. He's happy seconding the whole wall. He hasn't done anything like this before and I told him it would be una riesa, a laugh. I'm twelve metres away from him now and I can only just see him through this cloud. I have to fingertip mantelshelf these tiny edges. These Brazilians are psychos. I try once, pushing down with my fingertips, my back arched, wanting to put my right foot where my hand is. I waver. On the fence. My fingers begin to buckle and my feet skate back down to their little refuge. I stare into the rock and flex my knuckles. This time. I dig my nails behind the tiny edges, as if to prise them from the rock, and bounce my torso up and to the right, using only the rock's friction for my feet. Again I start to totter, metronoming back and forth, but now I push harder, stabbing the wall with my toes, arse out, sniffing the rock. I don't think I can …

He's still here, the doctor. Or has he come again? His syringe is out again and it is gigantic, towering above me. He shakes his head and says that all us gringos take too much of the white powder.

"Demasiado polvo blanco, senor."

I just stare and ... Aaaw! And then I can't ...

Make the move. It's my first VS. My skinny arms are tired and I'm holding my hex 9, the drilled-out one which I bought off PK. Trog is belaying me and he's stood miles away from the bottom of the crag. Why is this called the John Henry quarry? Who was he anyway? I make one last lunge, aiming for nothing in particular, and then I am falling. I clutch my new hex to my chest and I wonder if my original Moac will hold. Trog runs even further away from the wall to take in the slack and I land, bent kneed on the taut rope. I slide toward him, upside down, then I flip off and hit the heather. Behind the knee of my hairless leg there is a large wound. I can see the tendons like white strings and I begin to blubber, just like when I would run to my mum as a kid. Trog starts laughing. Guess I'm still a kid.

Shaking. I can't control the shaking.

Get your foot on. Stand up.

Rayo and Unai have left me some boiled rice before they went to do Llimani. I can't face it. Why have they left me? Such a long way from home. Home. Is that the derelict industrial wastes to the north of Manchester, where my blood is, or a sofa in Llanberis, where my friends and my rocks are? The dereliction is home. Can't get away from that. That's where I would go crying to my mother. But you're too old for that. The walls of the dark room have moved away and it's light and exhilarating and ...

I push with my leg and push with my hand on my knee. I rise in shudders and jabs, shaking in the updraft and then I am stood straight, on the tiny edge. I know I've done it. It looks easier ahead. I continue shuffling and still no gear. "You'll love this, Kiko." He comes across with a backrope from the others, laughing at me. It's getting late, the sun is low. If we move it we can top out before it gets dark. We need to top out if we want to ...

Get better. I just want to be better so I can carry on to Peru. If I can sell the rest of my climbing gear there, I can buy a ticket out of this place and hang out with my old friends again, see my family (this time I will visit them more often, let them know how I feel). I can hear Unai and his girlfriend having sex on the other side of this flimsy wall. It goes on and on and I stare at the flakes of paint on the ceiling, making shadows in the white light of the street lamp. I hear my Basque room-mates groan, "If he drank less maybe he would be able to come and give us all some peace." I curl up with more stomach cramps, my ten second warning …

The witch. It's the witch again. I don't want her in here. No more of your potions. You tried to poison me.

"*Tranquilo. Tranquilo. Vamos a ver tu futuro.*"

She wants to tell me my future. She's lit her stove again and she's melting lead in a pan. Now the lead is molten she pours it on the floor. She is sat on her haunches looking at me grinning from her big head. "*Kamisiraki,*" I say, my only Quecha word. "*Gualiki,*" she replies. The lead is set and she peels it up and lifts it in the air. She studies the frozen molten shapes, tracing them with her finger, and holds my wrist. She speaks.

"*Te vas a mejorar, Y te vas a llegar a tu hogar algun dia pronto.*"

I will be better. I will get home soon. Thanks, witch. *Gracias, gracias* …

We are below a chimney and the sun is burning again. I wipe the sweat from my forehead with my T-shirt. I move into the coolness of the shadows and bridge and back and foot easily upwards, though some gear would be nice. The clouds come swiftly back again, swirling hands fingering my passage. They take Kiko and the whole world away from me and I move as fast as I can to outrun their grasp. Into the light again. And back into chilly fog. I can hear something. Morena la de los ojos azules. No. That's not right.

"*La reina de las mujeres.*"

I can hear a serenade. And laughter. It's the Basques on the balcony. They're inside now taking lines and going on about some sleazy club they're off to in the centre of La Paz. *Cuidado*, guys. Watch out for *sucia policia*. The cops are bad news here. They took Kiko's passport off him the other day and said he couldn't have it back unless he gave them fifty bucks. The lad had no choice. The military are crazy, too … I am walking along minding my own business. A mumbling has started in the street. *El Terror, El Terror* they whisper. The mumbling has turned into shouts and people begin to panic. Street traders hurriedly pack up their jewellery and start to run. I just stand here and wait like an idiot. Then I hear the engine and into the street rumbles a yellow armoured vehicle and on its flank, in black, is painted EL TERROR. The soldier on top opens fire with his water cannon and sprays anyone who comes into the monster's way. I cower in a doorway and feel appalled at this mindless intimidation. I want to go home now.

The angle is easier now. We can see the top and we are cruising.

I feel more alive today. The guys are back off the mountains and I ate some more rice. Hope I can hold it down.

Look, I've found a metal tin. There's a scruffy little book. Let's sign our names in it. Ours are the first non-Brazilian names in here. Across the cloud forest we can see false horizons, one dome of granite after another stretching past the horizon. Our sun is setting and backlighting them.

Night-time. They are all bladdered and loudly asleep. Something's changed. I feel OK. No more possessed by that heinous virus. God, I'm hungry. I want cornflakes, cheese on toast and beans, doughnuts and custard slices. But first I need to shower the past ten days from me.

I hate rappeling in this darkness. I can never find the belays. The air has become heavy and moist and cold. Ten raps they said but I can only just see a metre in this fog. We have hit a terrace of spiky plants and it's my turn to go first. I slime over the edge and begin to descend. I have tied a knot in the end of my double ropes. When I reach the end of them I am still on a smooth wall. I swing back and forth in the whiteness of my headtorch beam, expecting to find a ledge but there's nothing. I am carrying Rat's rope, so I tie that on and rap again. Another fifty metres and still nothing. Guess this is the wrong spot. In this cold it doesn't seem very important to me. I just wish I had some prusik loops. I tie my shoe-laces onto the rope and begin to struggle upwards. It is boring and difficult. I tie the climbing rope to my harness at intervals so that if my shoe-laces snap I won't die. It's an hour or so later and I slump back onto the ledge. Iñaki has gone completely silent and is shaking violently. I question him but he won't answer. This is annoying me. Rat is the only other that has climbed anything big before so the two of us hold a conference, in English so the other two can't listen. "God knows what's down there, Rat. It could have been three metres to the ground or a hundred. I feel wasted now."

"Let me take over, Paul. You look after Iñaki." Rat disappears down a different route and I don't know what to do with our hypothermic friend. We huddle together and shake in our T-shirts. Then there's a shout. Very faint but we just hear it. "Come On Down Venga." I send the others and follow them to a ledge with a worn tree. This is the one, look, it's been abbed on before. Now there is more hope the boys buck up and in a couple more rope-lengths we hit the deck.

There must be a path here somewhere but I think we lost it long ago. There's no point in backtracking. We'll just have to keep crashing downwards over small cliffs and through spiky bushes. Bet this place is crawling with spiders and snakes at night. What's that? Eyes! No, glow worms I think. Get me out of here. They have coral snakes, you know. The most dangerous snakes in the world. Dead in seconds and this place could be crawling with them.

I can breath again. We are out of the undergrowth and into a pasture. Look there's the hut. I look up at the sky. The stars are out now. "Hijo de puta," says Iñaki. "Vamos a Bolivia." I couldn't agree more. Let's get to La Paz where there's warm beds and bars and parties. I've had it with these walls.

CHAPTER ELEVEN

A GAME ONE
CLIMBER PLAYED

I am lying in long grass, naked, I think, foetal. Warm. It's so pleasantly warm. I can hear distant cries. Children playing? I am adrift, going further and further toward slumber. I don't see but I feel I am surrounded by tall hedges. Insects buzz. Darkness begins to creep over me – my eyes are shut but I can feel it. Still warmth and a smiling comfort. Someone takes my hand – she must be knelt by me. I don't open my eyes, nothing need be physically gestured.

Then the hand slips inevitably away and I am left in a cavernous night with all the contentedness of a young child dozing in the afternoon. This is it, the most beautiful part of all my life. Utterly final.

"*Paul.*" A distant voice calls out.

"*Paul, wake up.*" Nearer now.

"WAKE UP."

Leave me alone. Let me sleep. Let me go.

"Come on, Paul, WAKE UP." My body is being shaken violently.

In anger now I turn to scold my disturber. "Why don't you just …"

… LIGHT – My eyes open. Someone has just thrown an electrical appliance into my wet dream and 240 volts are put through me. A blur. It's too bright for me to see. I want to ask questions (*Where am I? What the hell is going on?*) But it's impossible. I am just a single painful thought in a space of white noise. Then somewhere, below me and my thought, a body, I think related to me, attempts to breathe. An implosion of sharp points. The body convulses and is thrown onto its side. Lines, horizontal, vertical, diagonal. Beginning to focus. And colours, too. I gain some comprehension of what I am. *And colour!* A jet of red pisses out of my mouth and then a deafening sigh. Convulsions follow. More red water. Enormous gasps. Daggers are screwed further into my chest. *My chest!*

"Paul, you're in Wen Zawn and you've just ripped all your gear. You hit these rocks and then you went in the water. This is Glenn."

The words swim around in my head looking for a place to attach themselves. They settle in all the wrong places, though anagramatically they make some sense ... Glenn Zawn ... Hit the sea rocks ... "You've been wedged under water for about ten minutes. I pulled you out feet first." Glenn ... Gogarth ... "Glenn," I shout but no sound comes. Again I try to inhale the white noise but my throat will not allow it. Something stabs and twists. This is it. You've done it now. You've punctured your lungs for sure. Sleep ... Sleep. *Yeah go on, go to sleep and you'll die, you pathetic shit.* Is that me or someone else being cruel? I sob uncontrollably. My eyes focus now on Glenn. He's trying to solo up the wall of the Zawn. My whole body feels broken. Is it spread over all these rocks. "Don't leave me, Glenn." Still nothing comes out. Like a dolphin I dive in and out of a sea of unconsciousness. I want to continue my sleep, but my slumber is intruded upon.

"Paul, wake up – I'm your doctor and I just want to put this tube up your nose. Swallow as I push it in."

The sky, the sea, the walls of the zawn are stark white and ugly. The whole world is ugly. The pieces of my life are shaken through a sieve and the finer particles settle around me. My family, my friends, the woman I love. My body shudders in waves. I'm falling again but I can never tell if it's for the last time.

"Paul, it's raining outside. Let's stay warm under the covers. Let's stay in bed."

Am I this sad for them or for me? What a profound welling up of all the unfinished stories. The potential fairytale endings or the emotional farewells. From my right temple blood wicks across my wet face. It's still raining. My shoulders feel like they're in pieces. With each tiny gulp of air I inhale more panic. I want oxygen. Another time I slip into blackness.

"Paul, wake up – the stars are out, the weather's clear. We could be at the base of the Torre by 8.30."

Pain in back, in pelvis, in both ankles.

Glenn has dressed me in his clothes, but still I have gone beyond the shivers. From time to time the rigidity falls from me as though I am soaked in a hot bath. Then again distant voices laugh and shout. I strain but they don't come nearer. My imaginary saviours drift away. I am held.

"Paul, wake up." Glenn is slapping me about my face. "Don't sleep, it's dangerous." Now he's holding up a piece of frayed wire. "Look, you snapped a bloody wire. And the tide's coming in pretty fast." The bag of bones rattles on the hard, spiky floor. The tide could come in, night could fall, a storm could blow in from the west. I could slip out of my own back door and never return. It's not a problem for the bones. But it is a problem for Glenn. I hear him shouting. He informs me that five hours have passed.

My eyes hinge open. Above, the walls of the zawn are like the ribcage of some giant animal seen from the inside. The clouds are bent. For a fabulous moment my view becomes the cupola of Madrid's church of San Antonio, a circular sweep of Goya's colourful people against dull grey and green. The saint performs his miracle as the murderer slinks off into the crowd. The livid corpse I don't see. Over the railing San Antonio beckons to us down here. He waves. I feel important, at the centre of his miracle. They all wave.

"Paul, they're here. The rescue team."

Rescue? Ah! The cliff top. Adrenaline-fuelled ambivalence gives way to momentary excitedness, and more gulping for air. I hear the throbbing pulse of a helicopter and out beyond the neck there is a red boat which says RNLI. A dinghy speeds in and out clamber men without faces. As they lash me to a stretcher one of them asks me, "What's wrong? You've done way harder things in this zawn." I laugh. They are good at their job. I get panicky as I'm nonchalantly passed around inches above a clawing swell, all strapped up. Little gulps. Small gulps.

I am clipped into cables, winched up, swung around, lowered down, winched up again and pulled into a hovering yellow helicopter. The noise worries me. A mask is planted over my nose and mouth, a tap is turned and with a hiss my anxieties dissipate. The men grow faces. I shut my eyes …
A sloping shelf running with water. I can't swing my feet back onto the rock. I can't hold on any longer. I try to move up but I am strapped down. I slump back and relax. My body and the day begin to fit together.

I had wanted to reacquaint myself with the intricacies of climbing in Wen Zawn before attempting the big new line again up the back wall. It is wild rock down there. Unpredictable, untamable for some. You have to take time to build up a relationship where you and the rock can trust each other. I had been here many times, scared myself and forged partnerships. Conan with Dave Green, The Unrideable Donkey with Nick Dixon, Rubble (the softest route in the world) with Leigh McGinley. 'An easy day,' on the direct start to Games Climbers Play, I had said to Glenn. It went near the line of my project and we would have a good view across. We rappeled in to the foot of the zawn and Glenn got a belay about fifteen feet up above the lapping waves. Drizzle steadily fell. The moves began scary and awkward. I had to climb down twice before I could arrange some protection in clay/ rock mix. I started to move up, confidently, with all the inflated ego of a seasoned Gogarth climber about to plod up an easy Extreme. A couple more small wires, tips laybacking, then dripping hand cracks through steps of roofs. I was tiring but I knew how far I could go after I had hit the lactic acid wall. The belay was right there. Chalk was turning to mud in the cracks. I hung in there, pumping heavily and my forearms burned. I threw in a couple of extra Friends in case I should fall. "Jeez, Glenn, this is strenuous for E4!"

In the flared crack, fisting to the cuffs, I was faced with a choice; continue with deadmeat hands for six more feet and step across to the ledge, or move right now and grab hold of the same ledge. The decision had to be made in less than a second. I swung right from the crack and grabbed the ledge with my right hand. Water began to make little rivers down to my armpit. My feet cut loose into space, so I repositioned them on greasy smears and brought my left hand over. My error became apparent – the ledge was smooth and moist and sloped toward me alarmingly. I tried to mantel. No. Again. No. One more time. Utterly pumped I hung like a rag doll for a few timeless seconds contemplating the inevitable.

Without shouting to Glenn I throw myself off the rock to avoid falling badly. I am not too worried as I've got plenty of gear in, but I begin to accelerate. The horrid notion flashes across my mind that the cams haven't held and I brace myself for a longer fall. In the confusion I feel myself slow down imperceptibly and almost begin to relax. Then I continue to accelerate again. Instinctively, like other animals, I prepare to land on my feet. Ten pieces of gear explode from the rock. I land atop a sharp ridge sticking up out of the zawn floor and my right ankle crushes with the impact. In the same blurred moment I rocket head first into a narrow cleft of flushing sea water and stop.

And then I am lying in long grass, naked, I think.

CHAPTER TWELVE

ADRIFT

A bare room. A cell within a cell within a cell. Solitary confinement at a high angle. Under the interrogation lamp. Trickling salty sweat. Blinded by the light. Ball and chained by my rack of iron. I contemplate the pendulum from where I am. Riveted to the spot – on a ladder of rusty dots. Halfway up a clown's face, bending over us. With orange skin and black streaks where his mascara has run. Yes, he gets crazy and cries, but now he's laughing. The victims of his slapstick humour hold on, not getting the joke, getting nervy. Whilst the crowd below roars with laughter.

One, two, go.
No.
One, two, three, go.
One, two, three, shit.
One, two, go.
Again.
One, two, three, *no*.

One, two, three, yes, yes, c'mon, shit, no.

"Steeeeeve."

"Whaaaat?"

"I'm level with a spike. 'Bout twenty-five feet away. Trying to lasso it."

"Okaaay."

One, two ... No.

Two, three ... No.

What's wrong with the thing.

One, one, go. Why do I bother ...

"Paauul."

"*Wot?*"

"What's taking so long?"

"It's not easy, Steve, believe me."

One, two, three, no.

This time. One, two, yes. Ahaah. Yes.

"Got it, Steve."

"Niiice work."

Tie in to the lasso rope.

"Now lower me."

Come on, calm down, You can't hurt yourself yet.

I'm scared.

You're scared of failing in front of him. That's what it is.

But what about all these ropes and knots? I'm confused.

Concentrate on your job, man.

Swooosh.

The peregrine again.

Just climb the rope and prepare the spike for the pendulum, will you.

OK, the sling's on but the spike's a bit rounded now that I look a bit closer.

It'll do fine. You're just bottling.

"OK, Steve. Lower us, will you."

Why do I use 'us'? It implies that there's more than one of me.

"That'll do."

Perhaps there is.

There's only one of you. Now think about this swing ... You don't need to check your knot, you checked it ten minutes ago!

"OK. Hold me there. I'll get a swing going."

(From the meadow a wall-watcher sees a tiny dot, like a money spider, swinging left and right, left and right in a draft a little higher than some white bags).

There's an edge, an edge.

No, can't reach.

(The swinger's arc decreases and stops).

"I'll have to come down some more, Steve."

(The watcher's eye is still on the lens as the dot swings further and further. The watcher feels giddy just looking. The dot bounces out as well as across).

The edge – go on.

No.

One more.

One, two, three, jump … One, two.

One, two, jump … One, *yurs*!

(The dot stops at the end of its swing. Like an executive toy disobeying gravity).

OK, more edges. Free climb but keep the tension.

Sweat. Grains of granite the size of boulders.

"Keep the tension."

Can't go any further, I'll take a pisser. I'm level with the spike. It's miles away.

Get a hook on.

Fuck, fuck the hooks. Where the fuck're the hooks?

On your left, idiot.

Found them. *But the ledge slants*. If he gives me slack my body weight will be pulling straight down and the hook'll roll off.

Use two hooks in opposition then.

Facts like billboards.

That kinda works … *Phoooo.*

Calm down. Calm down.

There's nothing here, I gotta drill.

If you drill it won't be A5.

I can't climb A5. I can't cope.

Thudthudthud.

My heart sounds like the hammer.

Very observant. Come on you've got a long way to go.

He knows I'm drilling.

He would, too. What makes him so high and mighty?

Bangbangbang.

The hammer's become a limp fish.

At last.

Finally.

"OK, Steve. I gotta bolt in."

"Good one. Howzit look above?"

"More hooking then a ramp thing."

Hear that?

"Hear that?"

The girls

"The girls."

They've laid out their colourful clothes on the grass and their shouts harry to your fear.

"'Honeeeeee, wee loave youuu.'"

Do you think they heard?

"Yeeeeeaaaah."

They heard.

I want her. Couldn't they rap in to us or something?

OK, hooking, hooking. Yes. Stand up. And another.

"This is awesome, Steve. A1 hooks!"

Just hope I've drilled the bolt OK.

Or you're on for some granite rash.

Get lost.

The bolt's a way below now.

Smack a blade in then.

Steady. Or you'll rock your hook off.

How's that?

Vury Naaace Meesta Preeetchard.

I need a drink.

I need a fag.

"Just taking a break, Steve."

God, my feet hurt.

La la. La la la la la la. La la la la la la. La la la la la la.

But, I feel mad.

You're a long way from home, Sonny Jim.

"I'm going to start nailing up this ramp, but the placements are really shallow."

"I'll staay awaake."

Dingdindgingding.

That sounds OK.

Clip in.

Stand up.

Huh! Oh God, it moved.

Care … ful.

No sudden moves.

You're OK.

Another blade.
Dingdingdunk.
Not so good.
Watch you don't pull it out.
It points downwards, so if I lean out on it I can create a mechanical key.
Dunkdunkdunk.
Now my heart sounds like a peg being placed.
Another bad one.
This land is your land this land is my land.
Mmmmmm – a flared Friend slot.
Not so good. Only two cams.
Weight it.
From da da mountains to New York Island.
Dead easy.
This land was made for you and …
Snap.
Fuck.
Hold on.
What's happened?
The Friend's ripped.
Come on. Crimp like a bastard.
Gotta get the Friend.
Hook it with your foot.
It's slid away.
What to do now?
"Haaaaah."
Get moving.
Slap one on for that edge.
But that's moving further away from the pegs.
The pegs are shit.
Yeah, go on. And again. Side-pulls. Smear.
Wish-had-rock-shoes.
Heelhook. Brush the lichen off. Hang in. Dig the soil out of that hole.
Pull that root out. Go on. Get a nut in.
P-u-m-p-i-n-g.
Tap it in with your hammer.
Clip in.
Carefully.
Yes.
Another piece. A good pin.

Dingdingdingdingdingdingding. Ding ding.
Safer now. It's OK. I'm here. I'm here.
"Paaauuul."
"Yeah."
"Howsitgoing?"
"OK, Steve. Had a frightener but I'm back on track now. AAA111 to the beeeelay."

CHAPTER THIRTEEN

HYPERBOREA

To the north of the Arctic, beyond the tundra, beyond the vast sheets of ice, even beyond the pole is a land more wonderful than a mortal's most fanciful dream. A magical land where trees bear fruit throughout the four seasons and wheat is harvested in loaves. The land of unicorns, the abode of the gods – Odin, Tyr, Thor and Loki – known to the Norse as Asgard. The ancient Greeks called this place Hyperborea – beyond the north wind – and their boldest navigators went in search of a perfect life without toil or hunger. They never found their Hyperborea but this is the story of how we found ours.

At Denver Airport Steve and I sipped coffee and reminisced about the technicalities of our recent new route, Adrift, on El Capitan in Yosemite. The last call for boarding went by unheard during discussions about the UK Cowboy Lasso pitch and the Big Island Bivouac. And as Steve led up to the Illusion Chain our plane was thundering down the runway. After a firm telling off by the woman at the gate, we laughed at how we were so often untogether everywhere but on steep dangerous rocks, and blagged our way onto the next flight.

We had planned to try the Asgard Wall a year before. Plans rolled along haphazardly; many useless items were packed and crucial ones forgotten.

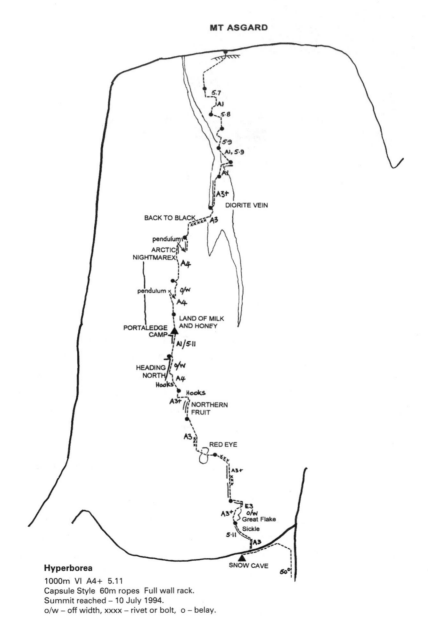

MT ASGARD

5.7
AI
5.8

5.9
AI, 5.9
AI
A3+

DIORITE VEIN

BACK TO BLACK A3

pendulum
ARCTIC
NIGHTMARE A4

pendulum x o/w
A4

LAND OF MILK
AND HONEY

PORTALEDGE
CAMP

AI/5.11

HEADING o/w
NORTH A4
Hooks

Hooks

A3+ NORTHERN
FRUIT

A3

RED EYE

A3+

A3+ E3
o/w
Great Flake
Sickle
5.11 A3

SNOW CAVE
50°

Hyperborea

1000m VI A4+ 5.11
Capsule Style 60m ropes Full wall rack.
Summit reached – 10 July 1994.
o/w – off width, xxxx – rivet or bolt, o – belay.

114

As if by accident the team eventually camped together on the windswept, boulderstrewn fjord shore of Pangnirtung. We met local Innuit people and got briefed at the park headquarters on how to behave if we got attacked by a polar bear. Apparently we had to run around the bear as quick as we could as they were incredibly fast at sprint starts but slow at turning. It was a desolate place. The people used to camp on the land throughout the year but in the early sixties the Canadian government undertook a huge pro-gramme to offer prefabricated housing to all Baffin's people here on the shores of the fiords. The loss of their traditions has created a generation gap and a new problem – unemployment and all its associated ills. In the supermarket the solvents were kept in a reinforced cage and to buy white gas we had to get a special permit from the police and take it to a sealed bunker where it was stored. Alcohol is banned, too.

Right up to the last day Simon Yates and Keith Jones had been working hard building portaledges at the Lyon Equipment factory in Dent and the day before Noel heard he had become Doctor Craine, zoologist. Just one week before I had been Steve's apprentice in modern hard aid on the vast sheet of El Capitan's East Face. And now, after years of picking up Doug Scott's *Big Wall Climbing* and gazing at that photo, we were taking a skidoo ride across the sea ice toward Asgard. Ipeelee, our driver, sped across the ice and towed the five of us on two trailers behind. Often we would come across cracks with dark water in them and Ipeelee would either drive around them or, if they were too long, turn around, take a run up and bounce across them. But we trusted him and, anyway, we were too in awe of the landscape that we were passing. The rolling hills had turned into giant granite slabs on either side of the fjord and, up ahead, snow-capped golden spires.

We had packed 1200 pounds of lentils and bigwall gear and this had to be moved thirty miles from the fjord head to the base of the wall on the Turner Glacier. There are no porters in the Arctic, so you either carry everything yourself or use a helicopter, which we resisted. However many plans we made of how all this gear was going to be shifted, the bags themselves seemed to decide when they would arrive at the wall. Dreams of hand cracks and stemming corners had overshadowed the reality of the workload. The idea of getting two people cracking on the wall almost immediately while the others ferried loads seemed a little naive. Food was rationed from day one and our loads never weighed less than eighty pounds.

As we crossed the Arctic Circle for the fifth time in three days I heard Noel comment, "Lord, every time I see those geese I feel less and less like a vegetarian." After the ninth day of load-carrying, our designs to trap the Arctic hare and geese had become elaborate in the extreme. The solitude was profound. Apart from a lone Catalan, who had come to attempt a solo of Mount Friga, we were the only people to have made footprints in the Auyuittuq National Park this year. Auyuittuq – 'the land that never melts'; the name was apt. None of us had ever known such cold. As we skied up the frozen rivers of the flat-bottomed Weasel valley we wondered how on earth we could climb in such temperatures. It was obvious, we had come too early and the land needed time to warm up.

Ferocious storms came on a whim from whichever horizon they cared to as we skied up the Caribou Glacier and became stormbound at the col. After 130 miles of hideous load-carrying we decided that never had an expedition reached such depths before the mountain had even been seen. The food fantasies. The girlfriend fantasies. Warm beds, coal fires and steam pudding. We spent two days at the Caribou Col as deep snow drifted around our tents. It was a welcome rest from the constant grind.

On the morning of the thirteenth day the sun came out and we peered down the slope which led to the Turner Glacier and the face we had come to climb. It was in dangerous condition but with so little food what could we do? We couldn't wait any longer and were desperate to see our line. Taking one of those risks that are accompanied by a silent prayer, we rappeled off the portaledge poles, lowering haulbags. The slope lay quiet and let us be. Roped together and dragging a haulbag apiece, we slithered down the glacier and our wall of dreams slowly turned to meet us. What we saw was both awesome and sickening. Huge patches of rime ice coated the face which was still very much in the shade at 5 p.m. The ice slope leading up to it was loaded and we all doubted silently whether, even if we got up the slope, it would be possible to take our hands out of our gloves to do technical aid work.

We set up camp and checked out the mountain, each impatiently awaiting his turn to look through the telescope. Panning upwards from the glacier the magnified arc traced a route: snow – scree – snow – buttress – ice – bergschrund – utterly blank granite. Working left and right the circular eye revealed only two cracks leaving the 'schrund on the whole face. This was disheartening but it made the choice simple. On the left a chimney led to the top of a pillar but above the wall blanked out. Further right a sickle-shape flake reached up to more flakes which died in mirror smooth rock. These disjointed features lured the imagination into believing that there was a way to reach the snaking corner halfway up the wall. The corner looked about five pitches long and above it a black vein of diorite led all the way to the decapitated summit. From previous experience of diorite we knew it would be loose but that loose, fractured diorite is climbable and blank granite isn't – without drilling.

Pinned down for thirty hours in another hoolie we made a pretty good guess at how many minute squares of ripstop nylon made up the inside of my tent. The next day dawned – I use this term loosely as there is no night during the Arctic midsummer – sunny and freezing and we attempted to wade waist-deep in snow up the lower slope. Breaststroke worked but it felt like a suicide attempt and we ran away sharpish. Back at camp Noel strolled to his tent and reached for the zipper. But it wasn't there. And neither was the tent. Luckily the tent's prints were all over the slope and we easily tracked it down a mile away. Steve shook his head in dismay at these displays of British incompetence. That night Keith make the soundest mountaineering decision of the day and broke the rationing. A noble *dahl*, fit for a glass case, as Tilman would say, was followed by pears, apricots, chocolate buttons, peanuts and caramel wafers covered in custard.

The following day was pivotal. Keith and I again attempted to fix ropes on the bottom slope but, instead of improving, the slope had gotten worse. Ten-inch slabs broke off in six-foot pieces which pushed me backwards as I tried to lead the traverse. It was futile. The snow needed a week or two and a good thaw to either slide or consolidate but, by now, Keith and Simon only had a fortnight left. Bad planning on the catering front meant we hadn't allowed for the huge appetites worked up load-carrying. We were already low on food.

The excruciating decision was made to walk the fifty miles home. We would shop and rest and stomp back in racked, ready and raring to go for another blast. And so, with our plan sorted, the pressure dropped 800 feet and we were pinned down in a blizzard for two more days. We met Jordi, our Catalan friend, on the descent. The reality of soloing a wall on Baffin had hit him like Thor's hammer, Mjöllnir, and he had decided to bag it. Noel, Steve and I glanced sideways at each other, cogs clicking in our heads. Wouldn't it be useful to have an extreme bigwall soloist on the team? "Hey, you come with us. Yes? *Ven con nosotros.*" He was delighted and joined us in the forced march to town.

After a very painful eating experience, and a farewell to Simon and Keith, we shopped and took a boat back up the now rapidly melting fjord. The boat couldn't make it all the way through the drift ice but the walk was easier with lighter packs and after three days of carbo-loading and power-lounging, we got pinned down by ferocious weather halfway to Asgard, but began to see a pattern of two days bad then one day reasonable emerging. We walked at night on the glacier.

Jordi's haulbag full of rope and hardware had been swept away in an avalanche. He was upset but "*Es la vida.*" From the base of Friga we looked across to the hourglass figure of the Scott/Hennek/Braithwaite/Nunn route on the East Face of Asgard, glowing gold in the 2 a.m. sun. This must be one of the greatest rock climbs in the world. Forty pitches all free at HVS (that's what Doug said, but Braithwaite reckoned more like E3!) and arcing a line with the purity of the Nose of El Cap. "Why are we struggling with this pie-in-the-sky wall when we could have done numerous routes alpine-style already?" These thoughts cannot be entertained seriously.

We got back to our ditch which we referred to as base camp at 6 a.m. after twenty-eight days of shuttling loads. We now had thirteen days of food with which to attempt a big wall. Chances were slim but we work for the means and never look to an end. With no time to waste, Steve and Jordi went straight up and, finding the slope in much better condition, fixed nearly to the wall. Noel and I went up later and got a rope on the last section. The fixed lines would make it feasible for us to hump our vast amount of kit up the seventy degree ice slope to the start of the route.

At the top of the slope we discovered the perfect advance camp to work from. The glacier-polished face arose, continually over-hung, out of a huge bergschrund banked with snow. This proved to be an effective catchment area for all the dropped gear. The outer lip of the bergschrund was thick and high and a good, safe spot for a cave. It would shield us from the wind and exposure and the constant reminders of where we were. I like to hide away in the evening, go home for a few hours. Then we touched rock. It felt like a symbolic moment after thirty days of labour and the agonies of migration. We joked about planting our Survival International flag right here.

I eagerly racked up, tied in and surveyed the start of the route. It was hard aid right off the ground. The first placement was a poor micronut high up, so I taped one on the end of a ski pole and, at full stretch, fiddled it in. Earlier the team had all agreed that there should be no falls on the route, as the consequence of an injury here could be disastrous. I swarmed up to the nut and fiddled for a few minutes, trying to place a Lost Arrow. Then the nut ripped and I landed flat on my back. After the hysterical laughter had died down I finished the pitch with the help of Noel's shoulder and a few skyhooks to bypass a three-piece suite of loose blocks. Noel moved swiftly up the next sickle pitch in one long fluid layback. This was why we were here, to climb rocks, not carry ninety-pound rucksacks up a downward-moving escalator. We fixed and came down.

With July came another terrible storm. This place was beginning to make Patagonia look like a holiday spot. But the weather cleared and the pitches crept by slowly. Beforehand we had decided on a no-drilling-on-Asgard policy but Steve, veteran of fifteen El Cap routes and new lines on Hooker and Black Canyon's Chasm Wall, knew better. Middendorf, one of the world's greatest wall climbers, had studied the face and commented, "Eighty holes at least." To the Americans, riveting blank rock is acceptable and I had become accustomed to linking features on otherwise blank walls during my Yosemite trip. On El Capitan most routes use up to 200 holes. The features themselves are good sport and if you want to climb them you have to get to them somehow. This was a new way of thinking to Noel but on the fourth pitch, as the rock blanked out, he was not upset when we pulled out the Californian riveting kit and made four holes to get from one flake to the next.

We began working in shifts. One pair would push the route higher, while the other two slept. After fifteen hours or so the teams would switch. Using this system, it was possible to climb around the clock. Our 200-foot ropes meant we could really stretch the pitches and we would, overall, waste much less time building belays.

On the fifth, red-eye pitch, Noel was learning how to drill a rivet ladder, engulfed in the swirling mist. Time nudged forward, sometimes stopping altogether as I lay in the portaledge drifting into unconsciousness and, occasionally, jerked back into semi-reality to feed rope out through the Gri-Gri. I took my boots off and rubbed my feet. Time jumped ahead a little. The bombardment of ice particles continued unabated, the odd fat rogue hitting me square on as I huddled under the fly sheet. And, suddenly, for the first time, I became aware of where I was. Not in India or on the Central Tower or on Zodiac. I was on the West Face of Mount Asgard on Baffin Island in the Arctic. I threw back the fly and looked out across a marvellous panorama of ice, rock and mist in the alpenglow of midnight. It struck me that this moment was the culmination of all that had passed in my life.

There were no shortcuts to arrive at this belay and even a minute's change on the compass could have led me a long way from here. Feed more rope out and light a cigarette. What if I had never met Mo Anthoine and he hadn't invited me on the Gangotri trip which got me started mountaineering? What if I had never met Noel or Steve? What if I'd parapleged myself when I fell at Gogarth last year? This lack of order makes me feel wonderfully insecure.

Time stops again until Noel shouts down, tapping home another shaky rivet into soft flaky rock, "I'll never confuse riveting with sport-climb bolting ever again." I shout up words of encouragement. One of the four or five insincere phrases pulled out of one's helmet during periods of intense boredom: "You're doing great," "Go for it," "Yeah," or "Nice one." While drilling the final rivet a shard of quartz shoots out of the hole and buries itself in Noel's eyeball. We fixed the rope pulled up from the ice slope and rapped back to the cave.

Noel's eye swelled up and we couldn't get the piece of rock out. He was in pain and we discussed him bailing out. We knew there was a doctor with a German team fifteen miles away in the Weasel Valley but Noel would need a guide and that would mean the end of the trip for all of us. There was too much work for two people. We laughed about his karmic price for debauching the rock but it was no joke. He might not lose his eye but the frailty of our plan was reinforced. Noel soon recovered but that piece of Asgard will forever be in his eye.

I belayed Steve on the double groove pitch. Easy nutting up the first groove led to a pendulum for a massive expanding flake. At the top of this the rock looked utterly blank. As Steve arrived at the dreaded blank section whoops of joy drifted down. At this point a knife-blade crack cheese-wires Asgard. We could follow it leftward and get toward the base of the main corner. After ten tied-off blade moves Steve headed up diagonally on circle heads and hooks and found a little foot ledge to belay on. What remained to the corner was a full pitch across loose flakes with big ledge-out potential. It was my turn to lead again.

'Heading North' was a sustained stretch of intense concentration and dubious mental games. It took the whole array of RURPs, beaks, heads and hooks to cross from one expanding dinner plate to the next and, finally, with monumental rope drag, I slumped onto a fine ledge at the base of the easy looking corner. In my dehydrated and fatigued state I was convinced we had pulled off the hardest part of the route. I couldn't have been more mistaken. Happy, I rapped off for a rest and left Jordi to belay Noel. He tried to free climb the first corner pitch but after a strong attempt reverted back to nailing. As Steve and I started the long rope climb back up for our next stint I felt a shiver and glanced up to see a black speck against the blue sky. The speck grew and I shouted to Steve, *"Rock."* All I could do, stuck on a rope as I was, was to watch the rock as it spiralled for a thousand feet, sailing toward me. It'll never hit me I thought, one person on such a massive expanse of wall. Never. But it kept coming, and then I heard it, like a buzzing sound. In the last seconds I knew it was going to hit me and I tensed my whole body and prepared for the flash that I assumed would come with death. I heard the impact, a deafening crack and then it hit me … But I was OK. It didn't even hurt. The rock the size of a house brick had landed on a small ledge about a foot above me, almost stopped dead and the rolled onto me with no force at all. Steve and I shouted up the wall in unison, "Stuuupid bastaaards," and from above came a meek, "Sorreee."

Later, in the warmth of our three-roomed ice house, Noel and I discussed the tactics employed on many free wall expeditions. We could have aided the pitch, left the gear in place and redpointed it at our convenience. As with the rest of the route, we could have chosen to free whichever pitch we felt like along the line of fixed rope. We had looked at Proboscis in The Cirque of the Unclimbables and were saddened to hear of its rap-bolting by two American friends. And the retro-bolting of the Pan-American route on El Gran Trono Blanco and walls in Yosemite. We decided that the essence of wall climbing was to get from the bottom to the top as efficiently as possible which, in the mountains, means as quickly as possible. But speed does not go hand in hand with redpointing. Most of Yosemite's big walls have taken the best part of a year to free. Free cruising is definitely less time-consuming than aid climbing but not necessarily more enjoyable. We didn't want to go back down and free lower pitches. We were looking upwards only and, besides, the hard aid opened up new doors of fear and excitement. Once the pins were in place we could have freed the first pitch at 5.12c. We would have got kudos of a hard free rating on a big wall but felt this would have made a mockery out of Asgard.

So with six days' food left it was imperative we should free what we could, dog what we couldn't and nail the impossible. Big wall free climbing does have an exciting future, though. The Salathe Wall of El Capitan and the Slovene route on Nameless Tower will get on-sight ascents but, to date, have any of these big wall media events truly been freed? (Since writing this Lynn Hill has made a fantastic one-day ascent of the Nose on El Capitan). I must admit it wasn't a big issue for us.[4]

We felt like the only people in the Arctic but presently four dots appeared on the glacier below. They left their haulbags at Asgard's feet and returned the next day with more loads. We knew they had come to try the wall but we had to bury any intrusion we felt. After all, this was one of the most sought-after unclimbed walls in the world. Perhaps it was the German team who we met on our shopping trip to Pangnirtung. They had with them a Hilti power drill and a twenty-kilo car battery. They wanted to make a route "that every-one could enjoy". We despaired at the thought of the noise pollution on our wall and future queues of climbers with only a rack of quickdraws. But use of the Hilti seems almost standard practice now. In 1992, whilst on the Central Tower of Paine, we happened upon machine-drilled bolts on easy ground just two pitches from the top on the German route.

---

4 Editor's note, 2012: Impressive big wall free climbs have followed the original publication of *Deep Play* in 1997. In Yosemite, Leo Houlding and Patch Hammond almost onsighted the route *El Nino* (5.13c) only days after the first ascent, and Leo has added other free climbs to the Valley in fine style. Tommy Caldwell and the Huber brothers, Alex and Thomas, are also responsible for many of Yosemite's new free climbs. The Hubers also freed the Wolfgang Güllich/Kurt Albert route *Eternal Flame* on Trango (Nameless) Tower in 2009.

The dots grew until they became full-sized Swiss climbers who had arrived to try our line. They were not too put out, though. It's a big face with lots of room. They would try further left. Steve set off on the eighth monster pitch, a snaking openbook only just split by a fragile knife-blade fissure. The fissure disappeared after fifteen bodylengths and reappeared four bodylengths to the right at a gross, loose, fat crack. Again the cold and boredom of my belay duty produced a transcendental state. The hours pass, falling with the avalanches which crash down the slabs of Loki opposite. It is night-time and the sun, weak yellow disc that it is, warms my face if I look square into it and shut my eyes. It coasts along the western horizon throughout the night rolling up and down the profiles of the mountain ridges and casting long shadows to the north, then east and south by morning. Now and again the ice falls. A small chip floats by and warns that we are in for a barrage. Slightly bigger pieces follow and then some very big chunks. Bugger transcendental states, now's the time to get cracking to avoid being taken out. As the ice blocks spin through the air they make the fearful whirr of aboriginal instruments that warn of their approach. The Inuit have a word for this kind of fear in the face of unpredictable violence, such as having to cross thin sea ice. The word is *kappia*.

Steve made the top of the first crack and, again, had to place two rivets from which he could make a pendulum into the fat crack. I feel here that, for the British reader at least, I should outline the distinction between riveting and bolting, for they are two very different things. Both require the drilling of a hole but rivets – being only a half inch long by a quarter inch diameter threaded nut – are body weight pieces for upward movement only. They cannot be considered as protection should one fall. After five or six hours Steve had built another fabulously exposed belay on blank over-hanging rock. As I cleaned the pitch the portaledge flew up the face like a giant black bird and at 3 a.m. I led off up the last rope-length in the open corner. Miles of brittle dinnerplating placements led to a disgusting diorite band about seventy foot thick. The diorite had the consistency of stale cake and would not be subdued by nailing. Only very silent nutting, *kappia* again, would get us through this delicate section which we named the Arctic Nightmare.

After twelve long body weight moves I found myself equalised on an RP2 and an RP3 behind a creaking cupboard door. Above was no place for a nut, so I tapped in an Arrow. Standing up in my aider I began to scrape a Walnut placement in the cake high above me. I heard a faint sound like the sounds you can hear when trying not to wake sleeping friends. The audible sound of taking the foil top off a milk bottle or turning a door handle. The Arrow slowly turns its hand from nine o'clock to twelve and the side of the crack falls off. The peg lands in my lap at the precise moment my right boot contacts a tiny edge and my fingers grasp the cupboard door. The door stays shut and I timidly weight the RPs. After some deep breaths and vivid pictures of home, friends and the future, I shout down for the bolt kit. In this soft muck even a bolt did not fill me with the warmth of security but it sufficed to finish the pitch.

At midday, after twenty hours of work, we slid down and switched with Noel and Jordi. They attempted the next pitch but became lost in a sea of dead calm rock. After some sleep Steve and I began work hauling a camp up the wall. It had taken six hours to climb the ropes to our highpoint, so we decided it was time to live on the wall. We had been putting this off as long as possible because our home-made portaledges – made out of a Lyon Equipment display for hanging clothes on – kept breaking whenever we sat on them, even at ground level. Keith and Simon had tested them for a few minutes, bouncing up and down in the factory. We also hauled food for five days, sleeping gear and a plastic barrel full of water. After the first night on the wall Noel and I christened our ledge the Potato Chip because of the pronounced twist it took on whenever we lay in it. The whole night would be spent fighting to stay in the thing.

In the morning we were woken by the throbbing sound of helicopter blades. It was the Californians, Brad Jarrett and Chris Breemer. We had met in Yosemite and wished each other luck. The helicopter settled them right below the mountain and within seconds had flown away, leaving them shocked on the glacier. We screamed to each other as Americans do and I pondered on what different memories we would each have of the approach, fantastic aerial views against a month of grind. I wouldn't trade places. I went up with Noel and finished what he and Jordi had started the day before. Our big wall soloist, who was going to lead all the hard pitches for us, was having a considerable amount of trouble even on the easiest pitches. In Spain he had led A5 but here he was finding A2 difficult. But he was good company and we were glad for his sake that he was with us and not trying to solo Friga.

This pitch was the key, linking the snaking corner to the diorite vein which led to the summit, and was sorted with hooks and heads and six rivets in blank rock. On the last move of the pitch I placed a fish hook and stood up to peruse the belay situation. The hook ripped straight through the soft rock and I was left hanging from my arms more petrified than the rock. After shouting repeatedly to Noel – after six hours your belayer can often be asleep – I let go and took the whipper. A blade held and I climbed to the belay with more caution.

On the raps back to the ledges we held a hanging conference with the other two and decided that Noel and I would get four or five hours' shut-eye and come back up. From now on we would go alpine-style to the summit. The weather had been gorgeous for a day or two and we were all aware that every good day was a day nearer the impending storm. Everything was going to plan. This just doesn't happen mountain climbing. After filling our faces with mash potato and Parmesan and trying to force down Noel's attempt at baking a coffee and walnut cake, a valiant effort in a portaledge, we rested a little and clamped back onto the lines. Steve's pitch was hard and soft but went steadily and, above, after eleven 200-foot pitches, the rock stopped being overhanging. We raced up the rope and congregated on a snowy ledge.

From here we could look straight down Charlie Porter's line. It is the only line on this side of the mountain, a superb corner prising open the south-west edge of the North summit. Porter was first to climb many of Yosemite's hard classics in the seventies and his presence there was a driving force in raising the standards of the day. The Shield and Mescalito and his solo of Zodiac were milestones in big walling but the crowds got too much for Porter and he went north in '79 in search of total solitude. He found it on Asgard in the form of an epic and painful adventure. Utterly alone he climbed the corner during two weeks of rain. When he got back down to earth he had to cut his boots from his swollen feet and crawl the thirty miles to the fjord-head. There he met some Inuit who gave him Coca-Cola! Soon after completing this magnificent climb Porter gave up big walling and holed up in Chile to work on an Aqua Culture project.

The sun blazed and we climbed as fast as a party of four could. Some mixed pitches and some free pitches on superb granite fell behind us. All the time the top was in sight. On Asgard there is no tedium of one false summit after another, you just slap the top and mantelshelf! I led a slow aid pitch and belayed twenty feet below the rim to give Noel the thrill of topping out first. We had to be very controlled and precise here as we were all getting extremely tired. Noel led up and free climbed through the summit overhang. By the time we had all jugged up it was 10 p.m. and the sun was shining low and bright from the west. It was an emotional time and after the handshakes and hugs we each wandered off on our own about the flat white field above the Arctic. To at last look east was special. Ranks of unclimbed Thors and Asgards marched deep into the distance. Out west the Penny Icecap shimmered in the haze. Noel shed a tear as Steve took photos in all directions.

Jordi spotted his avalanched haulbag at the base of Friga and I took my first shit in three days. As I squatted, I giggled at how lucky we were.

If the bad weather had continued just a day or two longer we would have used all our food and run out of time, but the window opened and let us in.

After a couple of hours on top and a good feed we carefully rapped back down the seven pitches to our fixed rope and cleaned that down to our ledge camp. We arrived at 3 a.m.; for Steve and Jordi it had been thirty-six hours of non-stop work. We had no trouble collapsing into a twelve-hour coma. When we awoke the weather was showing signs of change. A mackerel sky was shunting in from the west. So with battered, throbbing hands we began rappeling and lowering our kit down the face and staggered in one push all the way to base camp. The glacier had become horrifically soft and even on skis we sank to our knees.

After sleeping some and striking camp we shouted good luck to the other climbers and waddled out under hundred-pound sacks down the Turner Glacier. Black clouds boiled and poured over Loki. We tried to hurry but the storm had no trouble catching us. We were secretly glad that the other climbers were now experiencing some real Baffin weather. It would have been too much if our Californian friends had, after flying in by helicopter, got weeks of Mediterranean sunshine.

The long walk out is a blur. We fell repeatedly under our loads and I had the hallucinations I had known before that come at the end of an epic climb. The electric colours of the lichens and mosses made me stand, sway and stare but the feeling of an invisible presence and the voices were disturbing.

We met kind people who gave us morsels of food and at 10.30 one evening we met a small boat at the fjord-head and were whisked away toward civilisation. Noah and Joaby gave us tea, cake and cigarettes and we could only laugh as our boat stuck fast in drift ice only one mile from town. But we got in and that night were given real beds and fresh salmon. The people of Pangnirtung were celebrating because they had just caught their first beluga whale of the season. We joined in the jollity and entered the Inuit Olympics. After a long battle I won the stick jumping contest, as young mothers looked on with their babies in the hoods of their sealskin coats. And they all roared with laughter as Noel managed to whip himself on the backside with a twelve-foot bull-whip.

I can't remember on which long belay session it was, but I can recall the cold creeping onto the portaledge, numbing my feet, my legs and cradling my mind with torpor. I had drifted back to our desert trip only a couple of months before. Standing Rock, Shiprock, Monster Tower. We had climbed loads of towers and doing that allowed us to study the desert, from a distance, from up close and, unique to climbers and aviators, from above. The desert, the tundra and the ice of the poles may be the only places on earth where, at a glance, there seems to be nothing. But if you search closely the wealth of the land becomes apparent. There are vast forests but Arctic willow is only three inches high. The animals are so well camouflaged that they are difficult to detect even up close. Everything needs intense study, including the rock and especially if you are aid climbing. Examining the skin of the rock and trying to puncture it, not wholly unlike a sheep tick.

The history of the land is part of its wealth. The people who have moved upon it, the creatures that have evolved to live there, the angle of light that has pulled the same shadows from the boulders and pinnacles for thousands of years. During my cold meditations I too felt a part of the land and, by leaving our invisible mark, maybe we will always be a part of it.

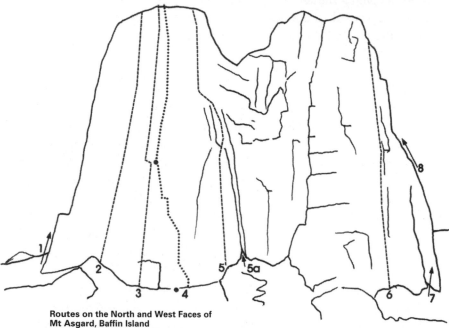

Routes on the North and West Faces of Mt Asgard, Baffin Island
Hd – Bolts or rivets placed by hand drills.
Pd – Power drills used.
US Big Wall grades employed where known.

1 Valkyrie 1994 Chris Breemer and Brad Jarrett (with helicopter approach). VI, A4+.

2 Inukshuk 1995 Denis Burdet, Cedric Choffat, Pierre Robert and Jean Michel Zweiacker. VI, A3+, 5.10+ (Hd) Swiss.

3 Nunavut 1996 Txus Lizarraga, Miguel Berazaluce, Raul Malero, Natxo Barriuso (helicopter approach). VI, A3, 5.8. Spanish.

4 Hyperborea 1994 Noel Craine, Paul Pritchard, Steve Quinlan and Jordi Tosas with (earlier) Keith Jones and Simon Yates 16 days A4, 5.11, 37 rivets/10 bolts (Hd). Anglo/American/Spanish.

5 Porter Route 1976 Charlie Porter (completed solo) with Rick Sylvester and Shary McVoy (for the first two thirds of the climb). One bolt (Hd). American. **5a** The dihedral line initially tried by this team following the earlier attempt by the Scott party.

6 South Face Direct 1988 Earl Redfern, John Barbella and two others. American.

7 South Edge from the West Flank 1988 Mario Manica, Fabio Leoni, Leonardi Luca and Fabrizio defrancesco. Alpine-style in 27 hours. (The upper part of this may follow the Lee/Koch/Wood Route). Italian.

8 South Ridge 1971 Guy Lee, Rob Wood and Phil Koch. Alpine-style. Anglo/American.

CHAPTER FOURTEEN

A SURVIVOR'S AFFAIR

I had arrived in Aragon and it was with a nervousness I felt

I knew well that I punched in the six figures. Why was I calling him? I needed to talk but I didn't know if he would want to.

I had met Pepé twice before. The first time, in Madrid Airport, I had noticed the expedition T-shirts and, like a spy, edged nearer to see where they were heading. Luckily the T-shirts weren't heading to Cerro Torre's East Face (where we were) but to La Catedrál. The next encounter was on a narrow trail by the side of Paine's Lago Nordenskold. He and Lorenzo Ortiz approached and babbled, their eyes staring somewhere above and behind us. They were escaping the mountains after completing a new climb, Cristal de Roca, on La Catedrál's East Face. Two months of precarious aiding, balancing around on a 3000-foot wall and jumaring fraying lines in awful winds would be enough to give any one of us the 2000-yard stare. So now, as the phone rang, he was a stranger to me but I felt as though I knew him. We shared something more than just the common bond of climbing or even the closer bond of Patagonian climbing, the shared experience of the wind and the waiting.

The telephone rang. Would he feel the same way? Beads of sweat broke out on the palms of my hands.

"Hola, Pepé. Esta Paul Pritchard aqui. Estoy en Riglos y quiero verte," I spoke in faltering Castillano.

Do you remember his big lumbering way, his utter motivation, his daftness and his smile? How nothing was ever taken seriously, how generosity wasn't a word in his vocabulary – whatever was his was common? How anyone would struggle to keep up with him on an approach? Philip said that on Torre Centrale he'd never seen a lead like it – out there on a vertical wall crimping tiny edges with the spindrift burying his knuckles. And … ? And have they found him yet?

"Yes, Riglos is wonderful." I hadn't said what I'd wanted to but I hoped there would be time. "See you tomorrow."

Pepé's full name is José Chaverri. He arrived at Riglos with his partner Xavier at 6 p.m. and, as they were off to the eastern fjords of Baffin Island in a week's time and he hadn't climbed all year because he had to work for the money to pay for such an expensive trip, he was keen to climb. So without hanging around (and in true Spanish style) they set off up the thousand-foot overhanging face of El Pison. Darkness saw them on the summit without headtorches – so we all went to bed, as they made the long rappel descent, safe in the knowledge that, although slightly unorthodox, they could look after themselves. The next day I was off the ground and we didn't talk. Well just once. "I don't know if they've found him either." Sometimes the will to climb is paramount. Almost anything can be delayed. This is understood, indeed expected, amongst climbers.

Sat in a darkened room the hypnotic click-click of the projector beckons us into Pepé's memories as they are cast onto the wall. He first shows his slides of the Kurtyka/Loretan and then the Slovene route on Trango Tower. Astonishingly, he climbed both of these routes in one trip, though for him these memories seem a little tainted.

"Too much fixed rope. On the Kurtyka dangerous snow means we don't stand right on summit and on the Slovene we forget our headlamps and get benighted only thirty metres below."

He seems almost more lackadaisical than a British climber but wears his inner drive on the outside. As he smokes perhaps his fortieth cheap cigarette of the day he informs us in dislocated English, "For make expedition the physical is not so importante. It is the motivation."

This talk of motivation and the click of the projector onto Patagonia makes my reason for coming here surface again. He had been mentioned now and again over the last few days but the mutual ice was hard to break. Teo – perhaps it's better if they don't find him. The memories flash onto the wall, each one punctuated by stark white light. Motivaciones Mixtos on Cerro Standhardt was their big new route together. Photos of golden granite glistening with trickles of water, front-pointing up ice-choked cracks. Immense, weird mushrooms of snow. For Pepé it was a departure from the siege tactics used on Trango and Catedrál. Eight times they walked up the miles of glacier and began the route, each time to be thwarted by storms. Teo's unwavering motivation and fine sense of the ridiculous ensured that going home was definitely not an option. Then, at last, after climbing the lower pitches for the God-knows-how-many'th time, they found themselves swinging past each other in the sunshine. In the ultimate lightweight style they carried no sleeping bags or stove, only a small bag of food and a spare jacket each.

A thick cloud of smoke is illuminated in the cone of light between the projector and the dangerously thawing ice formations of the headwall. After a long hard day where, to pay for the good weather they were receiving, the pair had to struggle through rapidly deteriorating snow conditions, they found a bivouac site below the headwall. Their clothing had become soaked after climbing through the meltwater and Teo had dropped the food bag. When light came again they warmed themselves up to another day of heat and decomposure of the mountain. There was only one thing to do and that was to continue. The 200-metre headwall was mixed free and aid on rock running with water amidst a barrage of ice blocks and always under the shadow of the grotesque and unstable summit mushroom. Like ostriches they minimised the risk by building belays under small overhangs. As the slides took us higher I pondered over the results of chance meetings between certain individuals and the dynamics which lead to such ludicrous schemes being undertaken. If fate plays no part, as scientists will have us believe, then chance is the most wondrous thing in our world.

On the final pitch as Teo aided on axes around the last overhang a few more molecules turned back to water. A fridge-size block of ice plunged down the wall and landed in Teo's lap, ripping every notch in his daisy chain, crushing his hands and tearing the muscles and tendons in the whole of one leg. With Teo's backing, Pepé made him safe and completed the pitch onto the summit snow. Then, metre by metre, the descent became a slow misery. Teo couldn't open a karabiner or shout directions and, occasionally, he would lose consciousness. No more slides appeared now. They had planned on rappeling the route down to the ramp of the original route, where they had bivouacked, and then descend, more or less on foot, the original route. As Teo could not walk, Pepé decided they would rappel straight down.

They had brought a very meagre amount of equipment for their light-weight ascent and were slowly using it all up on the endless rappels. Into the night they slithered. At the end of every rope-length into unknown territory Pepé built a belay with whatever kit they had left. Sometimes it would be one peg, in one inch. Twice the ropes got stuck and Pepé had to jumar up on unattached lines to free them. He placed their very last piton for their very last rappel and they collapsed to sleep out on the glacier. Pepé came round to find they were in a dangerous situation. Teo needed to get to hospital, he was hypothermic and his leg had swollen badly, though only twenty-one years old, he was already showing the mental skills necessary to be a survivor. Together they stumbled and crawled in the early morning light across the glacier to the Norwegian bivouac boulder where they had stashed food and sleeping bags. Ermanno Salvaterra, the Italian Patagonia expert had been watching their progress through the telescope from the Bridwell camp and, realising they were moving slower than was normal, had raced up to the bivouac to offer assistance. Soon they were in a helicopter heading for Calafate. That was in '94.

Pepé then talked about the local people who live in El Chalten, a desolate outpost at the foot of the mountains and, from the warmth and tone of his voice, his love for everything about Patagonia became evident.

"The rescue cost $1500 and we had no money. The people of El Chalten each put $100 to help Teo. He was well liked there."

An exhalation of sadness fell through the darkness, like the room had sighed and, momentarily illuminated in the stark whiteness, Pepé seemed more than his twenty-six years.

I drifted off to the Andean climbs I had made with Teo. The new rock climbs on La Pyramida above Bariloche. I could see him again on the end of a long loop of rope superimposed on the blue. Was Blood, Snot and Farts the best route name we could come up with? There were no such epics, though, and I felt jealous: I wanted to share the real intensity, too. But those pangs were dispersed as Pepé spoke.

"It was not as *un compañero de climbing* but as a life friend that I loved Teo. He is like a brother."

At first, when I felt the nervousness, I had no idea what we would talk about over Teo. I just guessed they would be important things. Big words that would make some sense of it all. In reality the words came out flat. The same words I had heard in a thousand movies. But later I found that if I didn't try so hard and just sat back and listened to Pepé's stories, that was enough. It is in those tales, shared and exaggerated, that our dead friends live on. Click.

"It was in '91 when I made Cerro Torre and Poincenot, and then FitzRoy with Teo. He only had seventeen years then."

The last slide was of a very large and very blurred limestone buttress in the Aragon Pyrenees.

"And this is where we will go and climb."

The alarm sounded at 5 a.m. I crawled out of bed hungover and cursing the fact that we had only had dinner five hours ago, but this is the way Pepé and his friends always seem to behave. It had transpired the night before that we were to attempt the third ascent of the 350-metre Pillar de Sobarbe on La Peña Montañesa which had taken three days to climb on the first ascent. During the evening Pepé had tried to contact Lorenzo (who had made the second ascent) to get an over-the-phone topo. He failed, so we would go with no idea of what might happen. After a high-speed slog up the scree slope in the darkness I was nearly vomiting and sweating heavily. We reached the foot of the route at dawn and I was shocked, as the buttress took shape, to discover that it was like 1200 feet of Stoney Middleton!

The pitches fell by and the rock was horribly loose – but these guys thought it was solid. This I couldn't understand and felt embarrassed after boasting about the intricacies of loose Gogarth climbing.

"The route is too good, no?"

They had another way of climbing to me. They just seemed to go all out for every pitch, on or off like they were sport climbing next to bolts. The long layback up the creaking flake made me nervous but they didn't understand my protestations. They went ahead and reefed on the loosest rock. A griffon vulture passed close and then rode away mimicking the drone of an unseen jet plane.

"*Aaargh!*"

I am awakened out of my enchantment by a loud deep scream. I look up for a second to see the blue sky above darkened by falling blocks. One of the blocks Pepé stops, but the others come thundering all around me before taking to space for the eight pitches below us.

"*Hijo de puta,*" he groaned and rolled his obviously paining shoulder before finishing off the pitch.

At the next belay we had a couple of hours to kill whilst Xavier led a long nailing and hooking pitch. Again the conversation turns to plans and past exploits. A couple of months before Pepé, with his friend Danial Ascaso (another Baffin partner), had made the first one-day ascent of the Torre Marbore in winter. This 400-metre mixed climb at Gavarnie, the jewel of the Pyrenees, is perhaps the hardest of its kind in Spain. The space below us seeps into the wall for a while as Pepé enthuses about the technicalities of free climbing steep snow-covered rock in plastic boots. He tells me of his Peru trip in '89 when he did the Ferrari route on Alpamayo and Huascaran, and of how he soloed Vallunarraqu and climbed Quitarraju's North Face. I inhale information for next year. We even touch upon the secret Peruvian granite big wall, and we laugh. It seems there are a few wall climbers around the world all with their imaginations churning over the same handful of lines on the earth's most aesthetic points.

Pepé is also eager to talk about the Aragon way of life. He displays a love of his land and a pride in his culture which gives me a sadness. It has all but disappeared in the industrial North of England, my home. But here also it would seem to be doomed eventually. One by one as the old shepherds die there are few youngsters who want to take their place. The ancient fiestas, mountain people tying chickens on the ends of poles or throwing goats to their deaths from the tops of tall towers, are less each decade. But the mountaintop monasteries appear strong and impenetrable and the legacy of the Moorish occupation cannot be taken from the land. As a mountain guide in the Aragon Pyrenees Pepé is expected to know about his territory and he enjoys learning more.

On the free-hanging prusik the void floods back out of the wall and becomes a sea of dizziness under my foot loops. As we climb higher the rock improves, as does, I feel, my friendship with these Spanish strangers. The last pitch goes to Pepé, skyhooking up pockets on top of the world, and we top out to catch the sun setting behind the snowy Pyrenees.

Despite the rush to get down in the fading light I made a moment of silence for myself to picture his big lumbering way and just to say, "Cheers, Teo."

Teo Plaza. An avalanche came and took him away on the side of Mount Tronador. Even though they haven't found him yet – he is still under the snow close to his home in Bariloche, Argentina – he is still curbing the future of his friends lives and affecting the dynamics of those 'chance' meetings. Plans will be hatched.

CHAPTER FIFTEEN

MAKING CASTLES
IN THE SAND

Here I go again. I lurched forward and fumbled with the zipper. I fought my way out through the tent door and launched vomit over the edge to watch it begin its thousand-foot spiral into the moonlight. Adam didn't stir. This was my first night at the shoulder camp (5600m) and I felt wretched. I slumped back, delirious, and felt icy water travel down my gullet. Lonely in the silence, I began to mull over the lessons I had learned so far on this trip and the lessons I was about to learn. I took out my notebook and scribbled:

1 ... on dealing with power crazed officials ...
The 45-degree heat in Rawalpindi lent an intense and surreal feel to the whole business of dealing with the authorities. Todd Skinner and his team, also heading for Trango, had had their appointment with the Ministry of Tourism just a little while before us and they came out with horror stories. Due to the secretary losing an important piece of paper the team had been forced to stay in the city for days longer than planned. When Todd commented on how hot the day was the head of the mountaineering division asked him if he knew how hot was the bomb that was dropped on Hiroshima? "7000 degrees. And do you know what happens to the body at

that temperature? Eyes explode, skin melts, everybody dead!" With this in mind we entered uneasily into the office. But our briefing went a little differently. We were allowed to go quickly but only after an anti-American rant. Then he thumped his fist on the desk and disclosed that he didn't just respect Britain, no, he loved it. We praised our luck and ran away to our hotel.

2 … on dealing with irritating reporters …
Again that damned reporter was waiting for us at the hotel. He wrote for a Pakistani national and hung around us for days. All he wanted to know about was 8000ers and how many had died on them. When he asked us about our climbing credentials we told him that Geraldine had made the first ascent of Lockwoods Chimney and that Adam had done a speed ascent of Mousetrap in two hours! He went away happy with his story and we headed for the mountains.

3 … on putting your life in the hands of others …
Driving the Braldu Gorge had more than a few moments of terror. What was described as the new road to Askole turned out to be little more than a footpath hairpinning its way across mud slides and deep canyons. We lost one jeep, because of an insane driver, luckily before we got to the really terrifying bit. The top-heavy jeeps skidded to a stop before a 200-yard scree chute. The porters dismounted, said some prayers and ran for it, stopping occasionally to dig out the road whilst being bombarded by falling rocks of all sizes. We joined in and afterwards the drivers put their feet down and went for it with the raging Braldu river a long way below. The key was to sit on the very top of the jeep (to ensure a quick escape) and to maintain complete faith in the inshallah factor.

4 … on the eradication of dangerous creatures …
Andy regaled us with the time when, up on the nearby Biafo Glacier, his team was plagued by a bear. It chewed all the cans, including gas canisters, and had to be fought off with fire. It was one of the last Himalayan brown bears in the area and over lunch Usup, a porter, told us proudly of how he had shot it dead. "Always eating trekker food and making trouble." Before all these trekkers and expeditions the Balti people had no real reason to go into the bears' habitat. But then came the tourists to create a bear problem. Andy and I looked at each other in disbelief.

5 ... on local beliefs ...

Many of the porters prostrate themselves toward Mecca and pray before undertaking anything they feel may be dangerous, such as passing before a loose hillside or climbing a gully. Watching a lone porter above the vastness of the Baltoro Glacier meditating in such a place of grandeur was a powerful scene which I will find hard to forget. I could equate with that need for a few moments' tranquillity. Myself, agnostic at this time, can still respect the healing of such a ritual. It made me want to construct my own.

6 ... on heroes and role models ...

On seeing Trango for the first time, thirteen years of sometimes hilarious, sometimes frightening stories and daydreams solidified. In '83, when I was struggling with VS's in the Lancashire quarries, two of my teachers in the arts of climbing and revelry, Ian Lonsdale and Dai Lampard, headed off to make the second ascent of a remote tower. We were all fired up by their enthusiasm. The guys got to within a couple of pitches of the top but then had to retreat in a storm after Lonsdale got his head stuck in a fat crack. Sometime after, I moved to North Wales, where I met Mo Anthoine who introduced me to mountaineering. He was on the first ascent of Trango with Boysen, Brown and Howells. That was in '76. Again the stories stuck with me; the rock fall in Tin Can Alley, Boysen getting his knee stuck and having to hack at it with a sharpened piton. Trango had become a subconscious ambition. And now, stood like a matchstick amidst these minarets, I felt as though I was in a house of God – the Gothic shapes and those echoes. You didn't want to make a sound. And over there, that one is even called the Cathedral, perhaps Gaudi's Sagrada Familia but on an incomprehensible scale. Until we made out the blue dot of Greg Child's abandoned portaledge on the Minamura route, that is. Then the whole place didn't shrink but grew larger in our perception. The famous Pole Voytek Kurtyka made a great climb up there too. Ever since my initiation into the mountains I had always looked to these two climbers for inspiration. And what was Kurtyka's comment after he had made it, with Erhard Loretan, to Trango's summit? That it took a greater physical effort than any of the 8000-metre peaks he had ascended. An imaginary voice with a Polish accent repeated the words in my mind, again and again, as I strained my neck to gaze up at the rock.

7 ... on choosing a suitable approach to the mountain ...

We made a base camp on the Dunge Glacier. After twelve days load-carrying in the Gullies of Hell, where we climbed only at night, like vampires, avoiding the hazards which day brings, we had a visit from some of our American friends. They happened to let slip that there was absolutely no snow on the Trango Glacier side of the mountain. We sighed. With most of our kit a thousand metres up in the gully we decided to stick with it. The women's team and Adam and Andy were trying to approach the Slovene route on the South Face and Noel and I were heading for a new line on the North Face. After almost two weeks of frying by day in our Gemini and gasping by night under pig loads of wall gear we were almost at the rock wall. Noel felt he needed some rest as the sun came up, but I thought I would continue with my load higher up the couloir. He told me to be safe and I assured him that I would be as I plodded off feeling angry that he was not strong enough to come with me. The ground was easy at first above our perched little camp on an exposed ridge above the Dunge Glacier. After a couple of hundred metres the ice became steeper and my bag of iron-mongery was weighing me down. I wanted to turn back, but I'd got the bugger so high! I know, I would leave it hanging on an ice screw and collect it tonight. Towards the end of the day it stormed and we sat out the night in our claustrophobic tent. I irritated Noel with my ability to sleep for long periods of time, as if mocking his insomnia. Avalanches raked our gully but we were safe on our little ridge. I began to worry about my bag of crucial gear up on the avalanche slope and my worries were founded when the next day on our way to the col we couldn't find it anywhere. What an idiot I had been, abandoning equipment in such an exposed place. I was amazed that Noel did not even begin to chastise me and felt guilty at my response the day before when he said he needed a rest.

We roped up and climbed in pitches up unstable snow and reached the Col Curran in the dark and, after tying our ropes together and making a long rappel, retreated to our little camp. At 5.30 a.m. we awoke to rain and wind and decided to run away to base camp and *dahl*. It should have been a simple descent but we had a little mishap. As I front-pointed down the slope for 500 metres Noel didn't emerge into the gully. I heard Kevin Starr of the American North Face expedition, who were up on their ledges, shouting. "Are you OK? Do you need help?" What was going on? I didn't understand. As I climbed back up the slope Noel's head appeared and moaned. It continued to rain and, as Noel crawled and slithered slowly towards me, he was hit by a slush avalanche. He dug in both his axes and screamed as I looked on useless. The river of slush cascaded over him and, credit to Noel's grip and determination, didn't sweep him away. Eventually the torrent abated enough for Noel to escape out of his rut and begin crawling over to me.

When we met he just spluttered, "Crevasse. Ribs."

"Don't say anything else, Noel. Let's just get you to camp." I felt terribly guilty – I should have stayed closer to him in such a dangerous place but hindsight doesn't appreciate the cold wet urge to hurry off that morning. We had no ropes with us, so I fielded him as he struggled down the steeper ice pitches. From his chest came a disturbing gurgling sound and I tried vainly to hurry him as heavy wet avalanches slid down the sides of the gully. Noel put a brave face on though, and after many hours we stumbled into camp. The whole team laughed when they saw Noel's familiar bedraggled form, they had no inkling of what had happened that morning. Noel burst into tears with the relief of the stress and our friends became more concerned. Donna, our expedition veterinary surgeon, checked him out by asking him to stand on all fours (the stance of most of her other patients) while she moved her stethoscope over his back and that was the end of the trip for him. Three broken ribs and a punctured lung. Andy, who with Adam had already fixed to the shoulder at 5600 metres, escorted Noel out of the mountains and home safely. So with only two of us left and my wall rack (including forty-seven cams and fifty RPs) lost in an avalanche we decided to go around to the right side of the mountain.

8 … on building sand castles …

Chasing these granite spires around the world, which is what I've been doing for the last five years, can be a frustrating business. A little like building sand castles – like the ones we built as children at the sea's edge. The tallest castles are very delicate structures and, like our best planned schemes, can topple before us. Sometimes you succeed and build a perfect castle but in time the tide always turns and your castle melts. Then it is time to build another.

9 … on dealing with military liaison officers …

"I will come with you on this mountain."

"Sorry, Captain Jamal, but you have not the experience."

"If a woman of forty-three can climb Trango then so can I."

Geraldine looked dismayed and shook her head. Captain Jamal had begun the trip as quite a friendly young man. We even bridged the cultural gap briefly and got him raving on the glacier. A full moon night, blowing his whistle and grooving to Leftfield and Primal Scream. But as soon as even the more absurd rules were slightly bent his humour evaporated. Growing up in the Thatcher age some of us had come to distrust and often view the military with contempt and now we had to work with a soldier.

Jamal found our liberal views and apparent lack of cohesiveness as difficult to cope with as we found his fatigues. That is not to say that he didn't have our respect and friendship but there was always a wall up which our concepts could never climb and meet on top. Ali and Ismail, our cooks, were good guys. They had turned our base camp into a garden with windmills and flowers and they always kept us happy with fine food when the storms lasted a little too long. We had to ask Captain Jamal to stop his reprimands and ordering them around. As the trip progressed our irritation intensified so much that his physical appearance began to change before us. He slowly transformed from a handsome boy into a bullfrog. To be fair, it must have been hard for him – his first time in the mountains, with strangers and for so long. But a little later something happened that was to make our captain even less approachable.

10 … on the extraction of bodies from lakes …

Mr Saki had tried to swim across the lake at the American base camp on the moraines of the Trango Glacier. He was their assistant cook and it was the eighteen-year-old's first time in the mountains. Out in the middle he had succumbed to cold and sank. He came up and shouted but everyone on the bank thought he was shouting for joy and waved back. When he went down again one of the Spanish expedition jumped in and tried to get to him but was repulsed by the freezing water. Three weeks later we had moved around to the American camp, from where the approach gully was wonderfully safe. One morning, when we emerged from our tents, we noticed that Mr Saki had surfaced so the LOs set about building a raft out of thermorests with which to go and fetch him in. They worked with childlike enthusiasm, like they were glad to have something 'manly' to do. Adnan, the Americans' LO, being a major, gave the orders while Captain Jamal obeyed, along with the cooks. When the raft was completed and the grim job in hand was imminent the awful thing happened – Major Adnan pulled rank and ordered Jamal to go out there and lasso the corpse. We sat down and groaned. As Jamal tried again and again to paddle out the wind changed direction and Mr Saki turned around and headed out toward the centre of the lake. Jamal paddled frantically turning round and round and then capsized. The Japanese expedition were capturing all the action on the three video cameras. Jamal was dragged in on our hundred-metre static rope and the LOs scratched their heads. As one of the women had suggested earlier, they then decided to use the blue barrels as extra ballast. Out Jamal went again, paddling with a snow shovel and with Adnan shouting in an excited voice, "Left a bit "and "Right a little", as if it were not obvious where the poor lad was floating. I remember a man in Llanberis lake who used to float up for just long enough to allow his rescuers to get near him and then, irritatingly, sink again to come up a few days later. Thankfully, Mr Saki stayed afloat long enough for Jamal to lasso and pull him in. With this ridiculous scene in our heads, and trying not to believe in bad omens, Adam and I set off up Tin Can Alley.

11 … on choosing optimum bad conditions …
We decided to go very light. Perhaps too light. We took one pair of plastic boots between us and one pair of rock shoes, one titanium ice axe and one pair of crampons. For a rack we had two sets of nuts and two sets of Friends, supplemented with huge Camalots. We had no pitons and no bivvy bags. Every item not absolutely essential was discarded. Todd and his team had very kindly let us jumar their ropes to the shoulder Adam had already climbed to. Here I spent the night vomiting and hating Adam for sleeping. For two days we took our time fixing four pitches above the shoulder, getting off on the feeling of climbing – something you don't do much of on trips of this kind. We were on an apron of glittering orange granite. In cherub-bum cracks sculpted by the ice and finished off by the hands of the wind. As Adam led us up a verglassed off-width on tipped out Camalot 5s, we fixed our ropes and, as the sun dogs and high cirrus had prophesied, in came the next storm. Down we fled. After an age of playing Nintendo at base camp we were getting desperate. All we wanted was to get this thing over and done with. The women had run out of time now and were about to leave and we wanted the same. Captain Jamal said he couldn't permit the team to split up but they had careers to rush back to and Adam and I were staying as long as it took.

"This is no way to conduct an expedition, Mr Paul. Things were going so well and now everything has fallen apart."

The glittering orange was fading crimson in the back of my mind. I was in danger of losing the magic amidst all this bad feeling. But as one day dawned the storm clouds had scattered and the altimeter told us to go. We waded through fresh snow and jumared up icefalls to again sleep at the shoulder. The Americans were looking weary. They'd been on this ledge for thirty days without going down. We packed two days of potato powder and stuffing mix and minimal clothing and jumared to our highpoint. As the sun came onto the wall we realised our unavoidable fate. Ice began to crash down the wall all around us, chandeliers falling in slow motion, and easy looking cracks were choked with foot-thick water ice. The sky was still hazy and we knew we only had a small window. It was now or not at all.

Progress was unbearably slow, like climbing hard Scottish mixed pitches with one toffee hammer. After our two days we were still 300 metres from the summit and very low on food. Adam made a terrible dinner of undissolved dried potato and my face was blooded after being hit by ice. We slept at the 'good bivvy' marked on the topo above a dark void. The third day dawned and illuminated eerie clouds. The wind had changed to a northerly, which we hadn't seen before, and the temperature steadily dropped. I started to have some trouble breathing and my lungs began to rattle – I just thought I was a bit chesty. I led my hardest pitch of the route, an overhanging icefall with lots of sculpting. The weather continued to deteriorate and this snail-pace was frustrating.

12 ... on choosing an able partner ...
Adam had never been proper mountaineering before and he found moments of this trip quite harrowing. This storm he found particularly worrying and he had suggested that maybe we should retreat. We perched on a ledge and had a brief conference. I was having increasing difficulty getting air in but was loathe to bail out this close.

"If you can lead it, Adam, I can jug it."

Adam is a master in the art of sloth and torpor but he surpassed everyone with his recent record-breaking speed ascents on El Capitan which prepared him well for this very situation. Now, on the sharp end, he slugged his way up corners and wide cracks with ease. When I arrived at the belay he would have tied-off the rope and be halfway up the next pitch. In this way we climbed hungry and reached a tormented summit which we could barely hang onto. It was 4.30 p.m. on August 13. A little later on the same day nine people, including friends, were blown off K2, just a few miles north, but we wouldn't know this for ten more days. What we endured for three days took three hours to descend by rappel. Sometimes the ropes would be stuck for just long enough to get us worried and then, with a tug, come falling down. Back at the shoulder the Americans met us with hot brews and food and I collapsed, more ill than elated, into the tent. I kept Adam awake all night with my bubbling lungs which he said sounded like I was smoking a bong.

13 ... on the collection of exotic ailments ...
I had never had pulmonary oedema before. It wasn't very pleasant at the time but it was definitely one for the collection. Now I have lots to talk about at dinner parties – of how, just before this trip, I had recovered from a very rare heart virus I'd picked up on Baffin Island, of how I'd got dysentery

in Bolivia, cerebral oedema in Gangotri, hepatitis in Hampi and now a dreadful case of bubbles on Trango. The next day I just wanted to stay in my pit and deteriorate but, thankfully, Adam forced me to get on the ropes. That evening back at camp, safe and almost well, we could now afford the luxury of laughter as our anecdotes, that will last a lifetime, took shape.

14 ... on luck and fate ...
A few days later, as we sit in camp eating porridge full of weevils, a huge rockfall rakes our gully and a plume of dust rises a thousand feet. We could smell the cordite. Mohammed, a porter friend, has just come down half an hour earlier with my abandoned haulbag. He looks up at the dust and then down at me and says with a grin, "Acha. Good."

15 ... on getting banned from Pakistan ...
"A Pakistani expedition would never abandon a leader who was dying from oedema. Perhaps these people you call your friends are not really so."

The head of the mountaineering division seemed to be enjoying this debriefing. I'm sure he was relishing toying with us, that feeling of power he must have been getting.

"Why did you not stop them leaving? You are their leader."

"Things are different where we come from. I cannot order people around, I can't force them to do things against their will."

"But the rules clearly state that an expedition must stay together at all times."

I tried to reason by saying that lots of other trips split up in the same way without any problems at all.

"But you were in a war zone. How do we know that members of your team are not spies for the Indians? How do we know that they were not taking pictures of important military installations?"

I almost giggled as I tried to imagine how those ramshackled groups of army tents on the Baltoro or those falling down bridges, that hundreds of tourists see every day, could be classed as important military installations, but before I could compose myself and answer he jumped in with a self-satisfied request.

"Please can you give us $400 for your abandoned equipment."

"But isn't it bad enough that I've lost thousands of dollars of equipment in the avalanche without having to pay more?"

"The mountain is not interested in how much your equipment costs. Now please pay and sign here. And could you please give Captain Jamal $400 for food."

"But the captain ate with us for the whole expedition. We fed him well."

"That is irrelevant. You signed here your agreement. Look, please."

The head of the mountaineering division held up a scrap of paper with my signature on it and smirked. He'd got us again. I couldn't remember, but I had obviously signed our money away in the delirium of the 45-degree heat on the way in. I despondently handed over our last wad of notes and then this man, from whom I was now trying to hide my frustration, enthusiastically threw his final punch.

"I am sorry," he smiled, "but you have left me no choice but to ban you and your team from Pakistan mountain climbing for four years."

We arose, limply shook hands, and left the office feeling well and truly stitched up.

DEEP PLAYERS

CHAPTER SIXTEEN

ON THE SHARK'S FIN WITH PHILIP LLOYD

There are always a multitude of reasons on a big mountain
for not going on but the most powerful, the one which decides
above all others, is the lack of will.

— Joe Tasker, *Savage Arena*

In September 1993 a small team of mates went to the Gangotri valley of
the Garhwal Himalaya to attempt to climb to the untrodden summit of
what we called the Meru Shark's Fin.

Few of you reading this will have heard the name Philip Lloyd. Why
should you? He was a beginner in life, only just realising what his body and
mind were capable of. Like the rest of us on that trip, he was only just
shedding the confusion of youth but still held a willingness to experiment
and learn. It was our first experience of high-altitude alpinism on a big wall.
We'd climbed 6000-metre peaks before but not overhanging ones! Some
of us were dealing with a new and radically different culture, reacting in
many ways – puzzlement, disbelief and outrage. New relationships were
formed. We met characters unlike any we had met before. We befriended
Hindu ascetics, pestering them for knowledge. We became especially close
to Om Giri – Mountain of Power – who lived in a cave and sat naked in
deep snow. We had the curiosity of children, living with open, seeing eyes,
senses linked to our minds, perhaps not understanding all, but willing to
absorb and ponder. Sponge and stone. And we had, it maybe, the naivety of
children; Dave decided that the slope was too prone to avalanche and, very
bravely, decided not to go. We saw the spire in the clouds and the romance

became entwined with the fear. And it exhilarated us, this climbing on eggshells. Before, I had sat with Philip in a forest in Patagonia and talked of dreams and plans.

"Trango?"

"Later." We could go there anytime, But Meru Central! An unclimbed peak by its hardest line. And we would try and free it. Naive? Maybe. Then I hope we never 'grow up'.

We looked further into the future. Trips to all corners of the world – Asgard, Dickey, Antarctica, the Trangos, Spitzbergen. The plans spiralled and I reckon we shared the same broad vision of what these trips meant. Not single accomplishments one after the other, but an urge to explore deeper and deeper. Elemental forces and toil. But the dreams of future adventures, which want to turn into granite plans, can, it seems, become as ephemeral as a dream in the dawn hours.

This is about Philip as a part of a team, on this climb and on others, and he was like us. We came from Britain and he from South Africa. He was a qualified lawyer but he soon found that the mountains gave him the food for which he hungered.

On that trip all was shared – the *dahl*, the load-carrying, the close calls and the exhilarating sights. How close we have all come – the day on the glacier when the sun was so hot it made our heads spin. I sat under an over-hung boulder which gave shade whilst Phil was on top of it stashing gear. When we came back six hours later the huge rock had toppled. We joked of charmed lives and good omens for the climb, but I chilled momentarily as I looked in the direction of Bhagirathi 3 and recalled my other brush with granite when a rock dropped hundreds of metres landing on my arm and ending my climb.

While resting at camp, we received a letter from the parents of a Spanish girl who had been swept down in an avalanche on Meru North. They requested of us that we cement a plaque to an appropriate boulder. Philip was alarmed at the idea of a plaque on such beautiful rocks. What finer monument than the mountains themselves? But the plaque was fixed in place.

And the shared sensations. The jumps in the cardiograph pattern which make a life special, load-carrying in the gully at night on those eggshells, trying not to wake the sleeping snow, careful not to talk too loudly. The torchlight in our footsteps illuminating crystals of snow, white electricity flashing over Shivling, breathing in moments of adrenaline too numerous to recall.

At the top of the gully we hacked out an ice cave in a peculiar spherical sérac that we named the hanging globe of pleasure. Noel couldn't make it that far because of his 'bad altitude problem', so he started drawing up plans for the LAMC – the Low-Altitude Mountaineering Club.

One night we talked of the past. I first met Philip in Patagonia when Noel and I were attempting the Central Tower of Paine with Sean Smith and Simon Yates. He was working, like others all over the world, just to finance more climbs. A collector of experiences rather than of things. But I guess the experiences collect themselves.

A sponsor said to me recently, "Isn't it about time you lucked out and got up something." You try your hardest, but topping out matters even less than the amount of experiences you gain. Phil had already climbed twenty big Bolivian peaks and on his days off work he climbed the North Tower of Paine and La Aleta de Tiburon which, coincidentally, translates as the Shark's Fin. We teamed up for some intense free ascents. Intense for the speed with which we had to climb and walk to complete each route in a day. How easy it would be to miss the climbing partner who complements your mood and skill so well. With this man there was no argument, no indecision, only laughter and swift movement.

I was fit then but I found it hard and challenging to keep pace with Philip. He loved to read Tilman. He was his hero and, like Tilman, he was hard on himself, as his uncle said, "allowing no room for mediocrity". Later Philip made an outrageous climb, Una Fina Linea de Locura, to the right of the South African dièdre on the Central Tower of Paine and a new route on the Painetta. He then went on a very adventurous winter trip to the Cordillera Sarmiento where he made the first ascent of the Fickle Finger of Fate at the head of the Fjord of the Mountains. With such strength, five languages and a law degree he became affectionately known to the Meru team as the Robot and every time he went to his tent we pictured him recharging his nuclear battery pack.

On the morning of our eighth day of upward movement on the Meru Shark's Fin, Johnny accidentally dropped his plastic boot whilst trying to get it on his foot. With the sight of a falling boot fell the vision of a summit ridge. Phil gave Johnny a hug and rigged up the rappel anchors. There was no place for anger over a dream which was misplaced in the night. Destiny can't be side-stepped.

An image flits by of the big man carrying two enormous haul-bags full of kit back towards our advance camp, whilst Johnny and I struggled behind with one rucksack each.

Back at camp, knackered: "Hey, Phil, I think we need to get straight back on this next season."

"Count me in."

Then he went off and soloed Bhagirathi 2 in less than twenty-four hours, camp to camp. Camp was about seven miles from the start of the route.

Who knows what the future would have witnessed. With him other climbers' dreams are lost. Dreams of repeating more Lloyd routes. There have been others in climbing's short history; John Hoyland fell in the Alps in 1934 at the age of nineteen and he had made some of the most audacious leads of the time on Cloggy and Glyder Fach. His peers waited to see what he'd do next but, like Phil, he never had the opportunity to face his limitations.

The team, as others, will always carry his inspiration and I will hold on to some of the stoic and perhaps sometimes dangerous refusal to be budged into retreat which only developed, for me, in our partnership.

Philip lost his life in December 1993 when a rappel anchor pulled as he retreated from the Towers of Paine in a storm.

He knew Paine.

CHAPTER SEVENTEEN

ACCIDENTAL HERO
– SILVO KARO

I've never really had a climbing hero. There's people I've respected, people I've thought crazy. There are people who've fired me up with their actions and I've wanted to emulate them. And then there's the odd climber from deepest history who perhaps I've credited with being slightly more superhuman than they really were. But there's no one great name for whom I've actually felt a nervousness about meeting. No one whose image (the image I have created) has elevated them above the other great climbers so that they have become 'obviously' invincible and their feats, their legacies almost divine. Well perhaps there was just one …

In September '96 Johnny Dawes and I waded around below a huge Himalayan wall, well out of our depth. Rocks whirred and whistled through the air like helicopters and bombs. Neither of us had been mountaineering before but we had come to try the unclimbed West Face – *thud* – of Bhagirathi 3. A rock impacted the slope nearby and vanished into the soft snow. The rubble was falling from the shale cap of the mountain a thousand metres above and the barrage increased as the sun swung around the sky to edge onto the wall. Pathetic little mites with a gigantic monster looming over them. Just as we had decided that our objective was inconceivable the whirr of one spinning lump of shale grew much louder than the others and I was smashed down the slope. Johnny helped me get back down to camp with a knackered arm and we both agreed a wall like that would be sheer suicide.

When we returned to Delhi we found the report of a Slovene pair who had just climbed the wall seven days before we had arrived. Straight up the centre, no fixed ropes – straight up the shale for God's sake. These people weren't like us. They must live at a different level of commitment, their skill must be complete mastery and, God, they must be single-minded. Silvo Karo. Janez Jeglic. Who were they? Since then the names have always jumped out at me from the pages of journals and magazines. Hazy black and whites of Cerro Torre in old copies of *Mountain*, dark figures grimacing out from the walls. That was them. As I researched my own Patagonian trips, I discovered that their names were synonymous with that wild place. Jim Bridwell wrote that the South Face of the Torre was the hardest ascent ever made in Patagonia, a place where I soon learned you can just about substitute the word epic for the word ascent. As you wander around the Fitz-Roy massif, Karo's routes stand out. The biggest lines on the biggest peaks. If, like me, you had read up on the place those routes dominate your view. The local experts, the annual big wall pilgrims from around the world, talk of his routes with a hint of humour, they are so audacious. Two of the routes, Devil's Dièdre on Fitz and Directissime de l'Enfer on Cerro Torre, are typified by great objective danger and are sometimes independently known as "that flushing Slovene death couloir".

In '93, whilst I was attempting a new route on the East Face of the Torre, we watched the avalanches and rocks roar down the corner line of his route every day. This just served to reinforce my image of this man's invincibility even more. I mean was he constantly dodging the rocks for weeks on end or were they bouncing off him? His name became a kind of joke to me and my friends. If it was too scary we'd "leave this one for Silvo Karo". Or if we saw a huge tottering pile of shale we'd say, "Look, there's a Silvo Karo route." His Eastern European origin added somewhat to the mystique, as here in Britain we have all too often lumped the Poles, Czechs, Russians, Hungarians and Yugoslavs together as another world of crazy climbers with no sense of self-preservation. I have even heard climbers bemoan the Eastern European bravery and try to demean their achievements: "How can we compete with psychos?" or "They only go for it so much because of the rewards they can reap off the state if they are successful." This attitude stems from deep-seated ignorance and is why even now many Eastern Europeans, even if they are doing the most important ascents in the world, receive hardly any financial help from the big companies. But somewhere out there was a man who beyond the mystique was only human, someone who took his craft very seriously. I wondered would I ever meet him.

The phone rang. He was here in Scotland and apparently interested in climbing with me. I began to feel nervous. Me and my friends laughed uneasily. What would he be like? Would his shoulders fit through the door? His hands must be like shovels. Imagine getting into a fight with him! I drove at night through the snow to where he was staying. On my way over a deserted moor I came upon an upturned car with its lamps on. This was turning into a surreal evening. Bricking it, I shone my torch through the window expecting to see a blood-spattered corpse. There was nothing. Phew! Then I began to have the ridiculous idea that perhaps these kind of events surround this man's life. Like climbing those couloirs, perhaps he saunters through his life while chaos reigns around him.

I pulled up at a remote house and knocked. I wiped my palm and pre-pared to meet a legend. I was led through to a room where a short well built man was sitting on the sofa. He rose and we shook hands. Just as I expected this hurt. "Hello. I am Silvo." He spoke like Dracula and seemed quite edgy. Without any further pleasantries we got down to talking of the big walls we had climbed in far off places. I felt like I had nothing to offer and every-thing to learn but due to his modest disposition I became less starstruck as the night ran late. I asked him how he had first come to go to Patagonia. He spoke slowly and with difficulty.

"We always went to Italy to buy shoes. Under Tito we could not get these things in our country. There I saw a poster of FitzRoy and I thought this was a most beautiful mountain. In November of '96 I went with my friends, Franč`ek Knez and Janez Jeglic, and we make a very hard new route, mixed. It was from the summit that we saw Cerro Torre."

I had seen the Devil's Dièdre, the flushing couloir. It still hasn't had a repeat.

"We climbed in poor equipment and very bad clothes," he continued. Up until recently Silvo had made do with fur hats, stripy Eastern block track-suits and 'Russian Gore-tex' (nylon).

That night we debated long over the Maestri affair. Silvo knew every shred of evidence for and against Maestri's claim to the first ascent of Cerro Torre. The debate was obviously one of his favourite cerebral pastimes, yet he wouldn't commit his opinion. I detected a dubious smirk though.

We arose at dawn to a puncture on my old motor. Silvo quickly replaced it with the bald spare and for the rest of my Scottish winter I never found a garage who could take it off to put a new one back on, so tightly did he screw the nuts up. After that his finger-strength became instantly legendary within the team. And so it was off to the Cairngorms, passing the wrecked car en route.

Below the Shelterstone we roped up and set off. Though feeling under pressure to perform, my pitch went OK, dot-to-dotting up clumps of turf on a protectionless slab. Silvo lead through, moving fast and determinedly. I watched closely to see what I could learn from his movements. At first I was almost disappointed to see him thrashing and using his tools so heavily but then it made me glad. Yes, he was 'only' human after all. Perhaps we could all aspire to these things … A hundred feet above me, with no gear in, he's out of sight. A barrage of junk snow falls on me and I hear a muffled cry. I brace myself on the belay and one of the two pieces I am on pops. I scramble back onto the stance. No falling body appears above me, so I frantically begin rebuilding the belay whilst those preconceptions begin to creep back into my mind. Maybe he is an Eastern European psycho after all … But the rope continues to run out steadily and I follow him up a pitch of hideously rotten snow. "Good lead, Silvo. Bad conditions, very Scottish." We moved together up the last hundred metres of our climb and clambered onto the flat summit. It was a rare, perfect day and there where people, scurrying dots, all around below us in the fresh snow, making the most of the sunshine. We smiled and shook hands.

"Our first climb. But perhaps not our last."

No way. Did I hear right? Does that mean that the great man might want to do a proper route with me one day? I could hardly contain myself as we sat and admired the view. I pestered him with questions about his life and his culture. I began to piece together a life story from his stilted English learned from base camps around the world.

Silvo was born in 1960 on a little farm near the town of Domzale, the second of four children. He grew up happily, working hard, caring for the animals and getting the crops in. "A hard worker will always make a good climber," he had said. His family lived in the mountains, so it was only natural for him to walk and scramble amongst them. He then went on to join the climbing club and begin the courses. I learned that the main work of the clubs under the communists was to take novice youths and train them to become mountaineers. In turn, they would train other novices. He progressed rapidly until, at nineteen, national service stole one and a half years from him. He hated the army and longed to be free to get back to the Julian Alps which he loved. Silvo then talked of his friends, his companions on some of the most treacherous walls in the world ... Whilst in hospital recovering from a broken leg received during a military exercise, he looked out of the window and saw a man climbing on the stone wall of the building. Back and forth he went repeating the same moves over and again. Silvo befriended him and credits the slightly older Franč]ek Knez with being the first Slovene to train and climb really hard moves. A little later a young Janez Jeglic joined the club and the trio made a tight group, climbing the hardest routes of the day in the Julian Alps. All their climbs were made with the pitons and wooden wedges all other Slovene climbers were using in the early eighties.

In 1981 the team visited America on an exchange. It was an exhilarating time. They used nuts and Friends for the first time. They saw just what was possible and had a chance to compare their ability, which was considerable. They were soon racing up the hardest routes on Devil's Tower, Eldorado Canyon and the Needles of South Dakota, making new climbs and first free ascents. On return to their home Silvo, Franč]ek and Janez turned their attention to Triglav, the highest point in their country. On consecutive weekends they made three new winter ascents on the 800-metre North Face, Silvo returning to his mechanics job in the factory mid-week.

"And then it was to FitzRoy, our first expedition."

We waded over the Cairngorm plateau and out of the mist appeared Sneachda. It was quite late in the day but I thought we could squeeze another route in.

"What are all these people doing?" Silvo chuckled and began snapping photos. "They will laugh in Slovenia when they see this."

"But this is the most popular crag in Scotland," I replied feeling protective.

"Why do they not wait for the snow to go from the rock before climbing?"

"It's the Scottish speciality. Mixed climbing. Don't you have cliffs like this in your home country?"

"Yes we have ... But we do not climb on them. Let us go and drink coffee."

Fair enough, I thought. Must seem pretty tame after the East Face of Torre Egger.

These climbers were bringing new levels of difficulty to Slovenia now, making routes that were unimaginable with only pitons or without the new found strength reaped from dedicated training, but Silvo was taking more and more time off from his factory job. This was frowned upon but, unlike other communist regimes, Tito's government wasn't nearly so oppressive.

In 1985, after an attempt on Kangchenjunga with a giant Yugoslavian expedition, on which Tomo Cesen topped out and Borut Bergant disappeared, Silvo decided he needed to take a year off to fulfil his climbing goals. He found his small-scale trip to Patagonia had suited him much more than the enormous machine of the Kangchenjunga expedition.

Not surprisingly, he was informed that if he took a whole year off work he would have no job to come back to. So he made his bed, and it was a good year. In November '85, after two months of fixing ropes and risking avalanches the three friends, along with an upcoming Slavco Svetetcic, Peter Podgornik and Pavle Kozjek made the first ascent of the East Face of Cerro Torre. It is an evil-looking route, Directissime de l'Enfer. I timed avalanches down it at one every twelve minutes! Silvo and Janez didn't know then that this was only the beginning of a long affair with Cerro Torre. July saw Silvo experimenting with high altitude again when he reached the summit of Broad Peak via the Austrian route. But that wasn't where his heart lay. Later that year and back on the small scale with his two old friends, he made what he describes as his finest route. Psycho Vertical, despite starting in the routine 'couloir of death' follows a dark thread line of thin cracks all the way to the top of Torre Egger, that slender hourglass of granite and snow that Don Whillans said looked like a newly opened champagne bottle.

During our talks Silvo never spoke of close shaves or epic retreats. It was like all his ascents had been executed first time, with skill and thought. Or perhaps the hard times were just part of the game – I was kept guessing. He seemed to prefer talking of his friends. They were close to him and he was as proud of their achievements as he was of others from his country. He liked to talk of Svetetcic with whom he made the second ascent of Rolling Stones (named for obvious reasons) on the North Face of the Grandes Jorasses in the fast time of one and a half days.

"Slavco could not free climb, 5+ at the most, and yet he soloed the Eiger Harlin route in a day and he went back to solo Rolling Stones. If he had succeeded on Gasherbrum 4 it would have been the greatest climb in the world." (Svetetcic disappeared whilst attempting to solo a new route on the West Face of Gasherbrum 4 whilst we were on the South Face of Trango Tower.)

That evening Silvo gave a slide-show in a local hotel. Despite the publicity, it was a small turn out. Not many people have heard the name Silvo Karo in Britain. Pictures of a beautiful land dissolved into one another upon the screen, unspoiled alpine meadows draped below the hulks of Triglav, Travnik and Sité. The film of Cerro Torre's South Face brought nervous laughter from the audience. Is this for real? But that snow is chest deep! They're actually climbing through waterfalls! The film made up for all the impressions that could not be put across with our lack of a solid common language. It said it all. And then a story Steve Gerberding told me flashed through my mind; Gerberding, a veteran of seventy El Capitan ascents and many Patagonian routes, was shopping in a crowded Yosemite deli when he saw Karo queueing up with a bag of bagels. Gerberding couldn't believe his eyes. He fell to his knees, prostrating himself at the visitor's feet and began shouting, "We are not worthy, we are not worthy", much to the embarrassment of Karo.

Sat on a pool table after the show, with glasses of dark beer, Silvo talked of his wife Alma and his son Jan. He had a sparkle in his eye when he spoke of them and recently he has given up big trips to spend more time with his family. He met Alma after his Bhagirathi 3 trip or, I should say, after his Everest trip because he and Janez went straight from their success in the Gangotri to attempt a traverse of the highest mountain. Not surprisingly Silvo was run down and developed health problems but he displayed remarkable will power. Since his marriage he has still found the will to climb hard sport climbs on the fine Slovene limestone and the hardest aid climbs on a family holiday to Yosemite. He also has made two disastrous trips to Bhagirathi 4, both times being thwarted by the Indian government's lack of organisation.

"Two times I pay for a permit and arrive in India to be told I cannot climb."

He was dismayed by the Kafkaesque bureaucracy which has to be surmounted to climb in India now and looks forward to trips to Chile or other easy countries. His last trip to India, with big wall ace John Middendorf, resulted in Silvo being banned from the country because, in frustration, he went to attempt the wall anyway. Liaison officers with other expeditions made sure he didn't get to climb, though.

I mentioned that we might get an early start tomorrow for a big day out in the Cairngorms and said my goodnight. It was a slightly later start than I had anticipated. After a leisurely breakfast and shopping for whisky, I eagerly pulled my equipment out of the back of the car. The car park was heaving with skiers in fluorescent clothes shielding their faces from the wind-blown fog. As I laced my boots up the great man, the man that never backs down, sat still in the front seat.

"What's wrong, Silvo? Do you feel OK? Would you like to go somewhere else?"

"I have seen enough bad weather in my life. I think we should go and drink coffee."

CHAPTER EIGHTEEN

A LESSON IN HEALING FROM ANDY PARKIN

Creag Meagaidh, March 1996.

"OK, so this is called a brake plate. You put the rope in like this and clip it through there. If I fall, which is highly unlikely, you pull this hand back and the friction will stop the rope running through. Just give me loads of slack, so as you don't accidentally pull me off."

Without another word I traversed off rightwards around a sharp arête and back into the gully. A full pitch of dripping ice lay above me. Grade V said the guidebook – no problem, I can climb fives in any condition. I was feeling particularly confident today, nothing could stop me. The first seventy feet was off vertical, pretty easy. It had a few patches of cruddy, slushy ice but I could soon scrape past them to the other patches of chewy thawing ice. I tunnelled behind a gigantic icicle for a rest and screwed a screw in. I couldn't see my partners. They were out of sight and I, as I later realised, was out of my mind.

I swung out onto the front face of the icicle and into the vertical. Ten feet of bomber Scottish ice and I got another screw which went in a little too easily and wobbled when I tugged on it. Oh well, I was feeling good. Great, in fact. I'd just carry on and see what came. I moved up into eggshell ice. My boots kicked straight through into the soft wet snow behind and my axes pulled out the odd time. I was used to dealing with this patchy sort of stuff and I could see a better looking area higher up. Limb by limb I crawled up the thin shell, keeping my chest right against the surface so as not to put too much weight on my arms. I was a long way out now … *Whoosh*. My body shudders and my heart starts to pound. The vibration makes my footholds collapse a tiny bit and I realise that it would be possible to come unstuck on this stuff. *"I hate jet planes"* I shout into the ice and briefly consider what I will write in my letter of complaint to the RAF. Dear Whoever: One of your pilots almost killed me on Creag Meagaidh yesterday blah blah.

Come on, get on with the climb. Each move now seems more insecure than the last. The eggshell is getting thinner and at one point I smash through and dig as far back as I can but find no purchase. The gaping hole I've made in front of me now makes it extra difficult to get higher but I manage, using a mixture of fear and bad style. Now I'm committed – I can't climb back down that slop. With my ice screw seventy feet below, it would be way too risky a manoeuvre. I stop being scared and start to feel a bit like a cardboard cut-out. There's a bulge above me with a reasonable looking patch of ice above it. I'll aim for that. I edge left with my tools right in front of my face, standing on the tip of a thin crust. I go up into the bulge. At a reach, I slam my left axe into the good looking ice and to my detached disappointment it shatters like a breaking mirror. I sigh and can already feel the bad luck descending upon me. I stay motionless, calmly having a schizophrenic debate in my head. One of me wants just to go for it, just start fighting. It's worked before, it could work now.

"No, stay still and wait for Nick to get around the top and drop a rope."

"That would take ages. Longer than this brittle shell will last."

"Reverse?"

"Is that possible?"

"Well, each move down is a move nearer to the screw and it looks even worse above."

"OK, down it is."

"This is a mistake," I say out loud.

I take out my right boot and go to kick it in lower down. As I swing my foot back my left foothole breaks and my body slumps down. I brace myself on my axes … But they start to rip. They slow down for less than a moment and I kick in my foot … Then they go. The ice falls away from my face and I throw my axes at it in one last attempt to retain contact. I knew it was futile. I remember beginning to scream, very loudly. Deeply at first, then getting higher in pitch. A mass of white flashes past my eyes, no slow motion here.

I don't touch anything as I rocket past my companions on the belay. I hit the end of my fall fully conscious and spring back up the gully on the stretchy 8.5. The wobbly ice screw has held.

"Are you all right?" Nick shouts from above.

After some time wheezing in a winded state, I look up and see a blurred Nick. I clutch at my, judging by the symptoms, broken body. "Why do I never learn?" was all I could say.

Moving through your small house I have to mind not to knock your belongings over. But you don't really care if they break. You didn't pay for them – you made nearly all of these things. You haven't said it to me but I think you have a clear idea of just how ephemeral all of this is. Like your stained glass mountains or the leaping salmon or, above the sink, Cerro Torre painted with a wall roller, the wire sculptures and the photo of the Peigne and Pelerins to help you recall your most frightened moments. Walking through into the front room my way is barred by haunted faces, crushed together, staring out at me from a large blue canvas. Kenya? India? Nepal? Where isn't so important. I can feel the heat and the clamour. It has similar aspects to the canvas you made in Hampi:

We dragged ourselves out of our mosquito nets extra early this morning in a futile attempt to beat the trickling humidity to the boulders. The rocks sat like giant potatoes on a broad smooth dome. They were already shimmering. We began to move excitedly, stiff from the long train journey which had brought us here from the cold granite of the Gangotri. There Andy had climbed Shivling with Sean Smith, while I had sat in camp with a knackered arm. In contrast, this rock felt to the fingers like the crust of a hot loaf fresh from the oven. We suffocated and traversed as local men made their morning ablutions nearby.

Andy set off to climb to the top of the first Hampi boulder. He had a different climbing style to the rest of us. His right arm and leg would always move first and then pull his thin ripped torso up a stop to allow his left limbs to locate the nearest edge or pocket. It seemed to me the movement of a very graceful crab. At the last move of the problem, as he hauled on a jug with his right arm, the rock broke and Andy fell to the ground. He was only a few feet up and for most of us a short ground fall would be no big deal, but for Andy with his fused hip the feline landings of a carefree youth are a hazy memory. He hit the bare rock with pencil straight legs and cracked his heels.

He didn't try to hide the agony as we carried him to a nearby café (many hardy mountain types would be ashamed to show such a weakness to pain). He began to retch as we fed him sweet tea and in the heat we all felt some of his delirium. A pair of white eyes moved in the darkness at the back of the room and, as they neared, a bald Tamil materialised. His skin was incredibly black. The man squatted at Andy's feet and, after much gesticulating, took the left foot in his hand and began his examination. We made room and watched. He squeezed and explored the heel and, feeling the pieces of loose bone floating, looked up at Andy, whose knuckles were now turning white in acknowledgement. Our man then moved over Andy's body, squeezing and manipulating every joint. Occasionally he would gasp in surprise and then assume a worried look when he fingered a bolt or plate under the skin. Slowly he broke into a proud smile. He had found an excellent subject with which to work. Then he tried to force the frozen elbow to straighten out and met with fierce opposition from a squirming Parkin. There, dazed and naive in all the heat and excitement, it is so easy to be sucked in by the many experienced con merchants but in the Swiss hospital Andy had felt the hands of the world's finest physiotherapists and quickly recognised that our friend, the temple masseur, had a gift.

Over the coming weeks our Tamil friend was to be Andy's constant companion, packing his feet in mud and administering herbal relaxants. During one particularly heavy bout of massage he pulled and twisted Andy's foot to extreme angles; "Stop, please, *stop!*" No effect. In a reflex response to the torment he kicked the man around the head and he fell backwards across the room. But he wasn't too put out – it was just the effect he was looking for. Andy was philosophical. He had spent so much of his life injured that he had a well rehearsed mental system for coping with such mishaps. He threw himself into his painting, as he had done before. The result, amongst lots of studies and portraits, was a huge bazaar scene on canvas. The many faces, like the faces in all Andy's crowds, look as if they know something. Something that not all are aware of – of course this is to my untrained and romantic eye.

Early in his career and on the Sheffield scene Andy had been a superb free climber. In '82 he went on a road trip to the States with Thierry Renault and made first on-sight ascents of many of the hardest routes of the day, including Leavitt's Hot Flyer in Boulder Canyon.

"All these blokes were saying 'Why don't we try this?' but that wasn't the way I thought. I said 'Why don't we do this?'."

In '83, after Lobsang and Broad Peak, he almost succeeded on a new route on K2 with Doug Scott. Then, in Cham, he made the first true winter solo of the Walker Spur on the North Face of the Grandes Jorasses. The Japanese alpinist Hasagowa had soloed the route in the late '70s but had resorted to siege tactics and fixed rope. Andy's one and a half day solo was made in a purist style.

"I wanted to honour Cassin and invoke some of the sense of discovery that he might have felt, walking over from Italy to make the first ascent. I climbed mostly free solo and without a route description. It was using this style that got me lost whilst soloing the Shroud."

The following season, whilst guiding on the Riffelhorn in Zermat, a belay failed when the rock gave way and Andy fell ninety feet onto a flat slab. The list of injuries was terrific, the most serious being a ruptured pericardium. I do not, and neither would Andy, wish to dwell on these injuries. It is better to dwell on the future than the past. This also goes for each and every route. Once a route is behind you (and especially with a poor memory) the experience may never have existed. The joy of climbing comes from the participation. Andy knows this and I reckon he won't be hanging up his boots, sitting by the fire and getting lost in reminiscence too early.

After the best part of a year in a Swiss hospital he was utterly broken. He assumed he would never climb again, and climbing was his life. He had hardly thought about anything else for years. This is the part of the story I needed to listen to. Then he began to paint. Mountains and people. The years passed and his body recovered. His choice of sites from which to paint became more adventurous as he moved further away from home and memory to find a suitable view. And, after time amongst the mountains, a desire to climb was instilled once again.

"A few years later I woke up and knew I was better. First I was a climber, then I was a painter and now I need both."

Now his painting and his climbing evolve side by side. Sculptures made from rubbish found on the glaciers form a significant part of his recent work.

"We found this airplane wreck on the Boissons and turned it into a huge elephant. An endangered species from human detritus."

In Patagonia Andy would spend days building cairns in the mountains or mobiles in the forest. He wouldn't take any photos and after a while the wind would take them back into the earth. Again the joy coming from the participation, and the mind looking to the next creation. That is not to say that Andy finds recounting past experiences disagreeable. It is the sheer size of these experiences, rather than his yarn-spinning abilities, that leaves me riveted. I was aghast when in his Chamonix house, he matter of factly told me of his three days alone, bivouacked at 8300 metres on Everest without oxygen or, more recently, when he modestly described his climb of Pelerinage on the Peigne with Christophe Beaudoin:

On the tenth pitch after lots of difficult mixed climbing Christophe took a belay and Andy led through on one-centimetre water ice.

"I was balancing on little ledges I was manufacturing with my ice pick to balance my front points on."

The angle was 80 degrees, unprotected and very delicate.

"At thirty metres I found a Friend on two cams and the climbing continued to be the hardest ice I've ever done. At sixty metres I still hadn't got another piece in and I was tip-toeing on verglas. There was no belay in sight, so I just kept going."

Out of rope, Christophe began climbing also. After a further fifteen metres Andy was on or off and Christophe was fighting desperately to stay on the face, now with even less ice after Andy had scratched up it.

"There was a spike above me which I couldn't quite reach, so I lunged for it. If I'd missed, the two of us would have gone. I just caught it. I couldn't believe the release of stress. I've never done anything like that – well perhaps on the Mermoz."

Patagonia has become a strong source of inspiration for him. For his painting and for his climbing. The depth and space of the sky and landscape are a challenge to paint and the frontierland atmosphere, the stories of Saint-Exupéry and the early explorers, have captured his imagination.

Andy's first ascent solo of Vol de Nuit on the East Face of the Mermoz caused quite a stir amongst the teams of international climbers camped at Rio Blanco. The weather had been dreadful and everyone was waiting for FitzRoy. Then one day, one of those kind of OK days that everyone knew would bag out before tomorrow, a lone climber was spotted through the binoculars picking his way up near vertical-looking mixed ground. Thin 90-degree ice and irreversible moves were again the hallmark of the climb and also a difficult aid section. As the young Argentinian hot-shots looked on, they commented with obvious respect, *"Andy es locisimo."*

"That climb was near the limit for me. One of those rare times when you experience that inner flight."

These recent climbs herald the beginning of a new era in Andy's life.

"I don't like to talk about that accident but these modern hard things I have done feel like part of a healing process to me."

These routes convey a level of self-trust and coolness of head that can only be achieved by someone utterly in touch with their body. And after being forced to listen to his body for so long this could definitely be said to be the case for Andy.

He settled his tumbler of wine on the table top.

"You'll get better, kiddo. That time I lost everything. I lost my girlfriend, she looked after me for ages but I got so down, so distant, that she finally gave up. I lost my mind, for a while."

I nodded, trying to relate all this to my own sorrowful state. "But if I can't climb what can I do?" I had a lump in my throat. I needed his help.

"As you get older you'll realise that climbing isn't everything. Other opportunities will present themselves to you and to grow you have to explore them.

"The next season I was in the Bridwell camp waiting for Cerro Torre."

When the weather window came he and his mate François began a new route on the South Face of "the hardest mountain in the world". The line they had chosen was a steep and technical ice gully and much of the climbing was on rotten crud. They moved swiftly to lessen the risk of being taken out by the band of séracs above. After a thousand metres they at last arrived at the Col of Hope, in plummeting air pressure. They made it to the Helmet ice formation when the storm hit. After bivouacking, they began their descent and decided, upon reaching the Col of Hope, that it would be asking too much of fate to chance rappeling down the séracs. There was no choice. They rappeled the Ferrari route onto the Hielo Continental, the Patagonian icecap. They had no food left and no map of the icecap. After jettisoning most of their hardware, days of walking ensued. They stumbled off the snout of the Tunnel Glacier and onto the Pampa in a hallucinatory state and kept going by eating dandelions.

I know it was all a mistake, but that's the kind of experience I have always looked for. Andy remembers seeing horses prancing around him, mocking him, and this experience provided the mental material for his recent horse sculptures made from wire or cut from sheet metal with a blow torch. After another day on the featureless expanse of the Pampa they met gauchos who gave them cooked beef.

"That made me sick. After nine days out I think I had done my internal organs some damage."

Andy showed me his paintings of the Torre. Before his climb the mountain had rounded edges and a classic mountain look with light coloured, almost warm, granite. And after, it looks brooding and Gothic. Higher, darker and sharper. That exercise showed him that the act of climbing a mountain can change one's perception of that mountain for ever.

The French chose to give Andy and François the Piolet d'Or award for the 'adventurous spirit' of their climb, A La Recherche du Temps Perdu. He had hidden the tacky trophy out of sight, but he did admit that the prize money would be useful for the forthcoming Alaska trip. Don't ask me how old he is.

Really he is ageless. For him there is no time to lose but that is not to say that he rushes and loses sight of the reasons for doing what he does. Amidst the exhibitions and commissions, the sculpting of human waste, the climbing and skiing and the planning of imminent trips to K2 and Patagonia, and what inspires me most, this man still finds time to revel into the night.

Summer '96

I've just finished my morning stretches, they take about an hour, and I move on to my mail. It's a little package from – Andy! A book on homeopathy. And a card:

Hey Paul

I found this in a book shop while I was visiting my mother. I know people who've had wonderous effects with it. Look into it, maybe it can help with the broken back and sternum. I'm getting slowly ready for the other hemisphere. Loads to do and life is buzzing. Cham is buried deep in snow and I've just started X-country skiing to get fit for sitting around in Patagonia. Leave around 8th Jan. Look after yourself, Kiddo.

Hasta la vista   Andy

AUTHOR'S GLOSSARY

of less common climbing terms

Climbing terms needing a precise definition and modern climbing terms or slang.
Plus a chapter-by-chapter table of British colloquialisms needing definition for
American readers.

abseil, rappel To descend a rope using a friction device.

aid climbing The opposite of free climbing. Using your equipment to assist upward progress and not just for protection.

alpine-style A pure style. To ascend as a contained unit with no fixed rope or camps.

ascender A clamp for ascending a rope.

barring Using your knee or elbow in opposition with your foot or hand to ascend wide fissures.

bashie, copperhead, circlehead Soft metal swages for moulding into incipient cracks to provide support for subtle aid climbing, though rarely strong enough to hold a long fall.

Bird Beak Oddly shaped piton for tapping into the thinnest of rock seams.

capsule ascent A compromise between alpine-style and seiging for big climbs that are too technical and prolonged to be done in one continuous alpine-style push. The party is self-contained using a camp or camps on the wall or face, pushing the route forward without returning to the valley.

crimp A small finger edge on a rock climb.

diedre, dihedral A corner feature in a rock wall.

drive in A type of ice piton.

dyno A dynamic move where the whole body parts from the rock to catch a hold.

EBs, PAs The most popular rock-shoe (French) until the early eighties when they were rendered obsolete when stickier rubber was introduced by Spanish manufacturers.

egyptian Turning side on to the rock to get more weight onto your feet.

Friend Camming device. Trade name of the first device of this type which is sometimes used generically for all similar devices.

Gri-Gri Trade name for a belaying device.

ground up, on-sight The finest style of climbing. Ascending a climb with no pre-inspection and therefore no knowledge of what horrors await you.

hand drilling Placing bolts or rivets by manual means. Ethically more respectable than power-drilling, particularly on big wall routes.

hook, bat hook Device for hanging on tiny edges on the rock's surface.

Jumar See *ascender*. In common with the "Friend" a generic term taken from the first device of this type.

jumaring, jugging A bout of climbing a fixed rope using an ascending device such as a Jumar.

nut A general term for any metal wedge (fitted with a wire or rope sling) that is handplaced into a crack or slot to provide protection or aid. Types include: Hexes, wedges, stoppers, curvers, spuds, Moacs, sliders, RPs.

piton, peg, pin Metal spikes of many sizes which are hammered into fissures in the rock. Types include: angles, Lost Arrows, blades, bongs, RURPs, knife blades etc.

portaledge Hanging tent which climbers sleep in on a vertical wall.

power-drilling Placing bolts or rivets using a power drill (either by rap-bolting or during an on-sight climb or by retro-bolting after an aided lead). This is increasingly done by some European and American big wall climbers to leave solid protection to allow pitches (that would otherwise need to be aided or semi-aided) on a big-wall climb to be freed by an athletic follow-up team and thus leave a climb more likely to attract sport climbers. Often controversial, particularly during on-sight big wall climbs.

rap-bolting Placing bolts in the rock using a rope from above.

redpointing Making a climb after rehearsing all the moves on a top rope and pre-placing all the quickdraws.

retro-bolting The adding of bolts to a climb after the first ascent. Considered ethically unacceptable by most climbers.

rivet Small metal pin driven into a shallow drilled hole for artificially climbing blank rock. Quicker and more lightweight than fixing a bolt on an aid climb and, providing it is done sparingly, it is presently thought to be visually and ethically preferable than equipping blank passages with bolt ladders.

sieging Climbing a route from a secure base camp, with repeated ascents and descents (sometimes with intermediate camps) to and from the high point to push the climb forward. Less committing than an alpine-style or even a capsule-style ascent.

skyhook Steel hook for hanging on a rock edge. Usually for aid climbing but also used on Wales's most dangerous free climbs.
slap Dynamic lunge for a hold.
sport climbing Convenient, safe climbing with drilled bolts for protection. A derivation from proper climbing – initially an attempt by normal climbers to push standards but soon evolved into a broader movement to process rock-climbing into a more athletically orientated, sanitised and measurable procedure by removing its main dangers and logistical complexities. Controversial, except on some (not all) extremely overhanging and crackless cliffs that are difficult or impossible to free-climb by other means. In other circumstances it is thought by many to represent a threat to the uncertainty and adventure of the cliffs that lies at the centre of making climbing a uniquely rewarding pastime. Dates from the easy availability of cordless drills which made such climbs feasible to establish. Supported by a growth in guiding, hut wardens, manufacturers, media and educational interest in the commercial exploitation of rock activity. Environmentally destructive.

CHAPTER 1
"bricking it" – scared stiff
"paggered" – beaten up or punched or feeling that way
"spends" – money available for spending
Youth Training Scheme – Government scheme to gainfully occupy the young unemployed

CHAPTER 2
"fifties for the leccy meter" – 50 pence pieces required for a pay-as-you-use electricity meter
"lashed up" – drunk, intoxicated
tannoy – loudspeaker in a factory or other crowded location
Giros – Government cheques issued (on the Giro Bank) to registered unemployed
"skint" – out of money, stony broke

CHAPTER 3
"Gobsmacked" – stunned, surprised or amazed (usually about something nice)

CHAPTER 4
"hacked" – getting there fast
"knackered" (as in a car being knackered, or even a person) – totally used up, tired, utterly spent (derived from Knacker – one who buys and slaughters spent horses)
"get a ton out" – squeezing 100mph out of a car
"ceilidh" – a Scottish dance and drinks party usually with accordion music

CHAPTER 6
"Wendy house" – a play house big enough for children to enter
MEF – Mount Everest Foundation based at the:
RGS – the Royal Geographical Society in London
"barny" – an argument or private row

CHAPTER 8
"gurning" – pulling a face sometimes through a horse bridle (an old Devonian custom)

CHAPTER 9
Wackford Squeers – a route named after the headmaster in Dickens's "Nicholas Nickleby"
Moac – an early and classic British nut design, a slender four-faceted wedge

CHAPTER 12
"bottling" (abbr. from "bottling-out") – running out of courage, "bottle" being a cockney term for courage

CHAPTER 13
"hoolie" – a strong wind

CHAPTER 14
Gemini – a make of bivouac tent

NOTES ABOUT THE ESSAYS

FIRE-STARTER. The gritstone quarries of Bolton are dismal places but to me they were everything. Since my childhood, I have always felt summoned to such places of industrial dereliction to practise my art or simply to explore the past. Previously unpublished.

RUBBLE MERCHANTS, SLATEHEADS AND OTHERS. I moved to that capital of British climbing, Llanberis, in 1986 to follow the path of full time climber. It is both fortunate and unfortunate that things can't always stay the same. *On the Edge* 69 (1997).

LOST IN THE BROCCOLI GARDEN. Gogarth epitomises British sea cliff climbing. When you make contact with the rock you can feel the history seeping into your fingers. I have loved Gogarth and I have hated the place. I feel I grew up a little on the Red Walls. *High* (1987).

A PIECE OF DRIFTWOOD. Ed Stone was part of a close-knit team of friends in Llanberis who shared many good times. He died solo climbing on the Trinity face of Yr Wyddfa in 1994. Previously unpublished.

ON THE BIG STONE. The first of many trips to Sron Ulladale. I later climbed Knuckle Sandwich (E7) with Johnny and Moskill Grooves (E6) with Johnny and Ben Moon. Ten years later the Scoop has been climbed in a day, but with pitons in-situ and a description of where the climb goes, it is a much more feasible proposition. *On the Edge* 49 (1995).

BHAGIRATHI DIARY. In 1990 I went on my first mountain climbing 'expedition' with Johnny Dawes, Joe Simpson and Bob Drury. We travelled in tandem with another British team who were attempting Shivling and made a feeble attempt on Bhagirathi 3. It was all so new to me, Bob and Johnny and we set about the task of organising a big expedition with enthusiasm. Now, a few years later, it's difficult to recapture that magic. Expeditions are now called holidays and though I need them I have a more relaxed approach. Previously unpublished.

EL REGALO DE MWONO. My first big wall climbing experience and the beginning of a nine-month road trip. I forsake the Yosemite training and jumped in at the deep end. The route is 1200m long and the grade is 6, 5.11, A4 and Scottish ice V. Team members were Noel Craine, Sean Smith, Simon Yates, Hanneke Steenmetz and myself. *American Alpine Journal* (1993).

EL CABALLO DE DIABLO. The best free climb I ever made was marred by feelings of guilt. This climb means more to me, perhaps, than any other. The day, the company, the style of ascent, everything gelled to make the perfect climb. The descent was another story, a story from which I learnt a few lessons. To me it is sadly ironic that Philip should have later died on this mountain. We graded the climb ED+, E5, French 7A, 550m. *On the Edge* 59 (1996).

JUST PASSING THROUGH. Another stop on a long journey through South America. *On the Edge* 61 (1996).

THE DOCTOR AND THE WITCH. In 1992, whilst feeling homesick in Bolivia, I went down with amoebic dysentery. I had just arrived from Brazil where my Basque, Catalonian and Argentinian friends and I had made a fabulous wall climb. In my fever the present and the near past became intertwined. *On the Edge* 65 (1997).

A GAME ONE CLIMBER PLAYED. In 1993 I came unstuck at Gogarth whilst trying to make the second ascent of Pat Littlejohn's direct start to Games Climbers Play. My Australian friend, and partner for the day, Glenn Robbins, pulled me out of the water, resuscitated me and sat with me for three hours until Oliver Saunders, who was out walking, happened to pass by. Glenn shouted to him and he ran to call a rescue. *Mountain Yodel* 6 (1997).

NOTES ABOUT THE ESSAYS

ADRIFT. In May 1994, with Steve Quinlan, I climbed a new line on the East face of El Capitan, Yosemite. The essence of the climb for me was here, on the UK Cowboy pitch. We got down off the climb and headed straight to Baffin Island. Grade 6, A4, 5.9, 1000m. *On the Edge* 60 (1996).

HYPERBOREA. Asgard West Face, 1994. Simon Yates, Sean Smith, Keith Jones, Steve Quinlan, Noel Craine, Jordi Tosas, Paul Pritchard. Grade 6, A4, E4. 1000m. *On the Edge* 45 (1994).

A SURVIVOR'S AFFAIR. Teo Plaza died in an avalanche on El Tronador with other friends whilst training to become an Argentinian guide. He was the most talented of the young Bariloche set. *On the Edge* 50 (1995).

MAKING CASTLES IN THE SAND. Trango Tower mixed men and women's expedition 1995. Donna Claridge, Celia Bull, Geraldine Westrupp, Kate Phillips, Noel Craine, Adam Wainwright, Andy Cave, Paul Pritchard, Ali Hussain Abadi, Ismael Bondo, Captain Jamal Mohammed. The Slovene route is 1000m long and has been free climbed in fine style by Wolfgang Güllich and Kurt Albert and later, for a film, by Catherine Destivelle and Jeff Lowe. The grade was 5.12b. With ice in the cracks we were forced to use some aid and for us the grade stood at 6, 5.10, A2. The first ascent was made in 1984 by Franček Knez, S. Canker and B. Srot. *On the Edge* 53 (1995).

ON THE SHARK'S FIN WITH PHILIP LLOYD. In 1993 Philip Lloyd, Johnny Dawes and I tried to climb the Meru Shark's Fin in Gangotri. We were repulsed after Johnny accidentally dropped his boot whilst trying to get it on after a bivouac one morning. A reminiscence of my last time with Philip. *Mountain Review* 7 (1994).

ACCIDENTAL HERO – SILVO KARO. A tough man from a tough world. An inspiration. *On the Edge* 58 (1996).

A LESSON IN HEALING FROM ANDY PARKIN. On Centre Post Direct Finish I came unstuck and fell 50 metres sustaining four crushed vertebrae, a broken sternum and a fractured skull. Nick Kekus lowered me and four clients down a thousand feet of gully and stayed with me while the others went to call for a helicopter. From Andy I learnt how to re-build life (and maintain sanity) when all seemed devastated by injury and illness. A combination of articles in *On the Edge* 48 and 57.

Note: Most of the articles have been substantially edited and developed since their first publication.